Excel 5

by Jennifer Fulton and Joe Kraynak

GW00727929

alpha
books

A Division of Prentice Hall Computer Publishing

201 W. 103rd Street, Indianapolis, Indiana 46290 USA

To Maria: Thank you for your encouragement and for making me feel so welcome in my new family. —Jennifer

© 1993 by Alpha Books

International Standard Book Number: 1-56761-316-0
Library of Congress Catalog Card Number: 93-72162

96   95   94   93   8   7   6   5   4   3   2   1

Interpretation of the printing code: the rightmost number of the first series of numbers is the year of the book's printing; the rightmost number of the second series of numbers is the number of the book's printing. For example, a printing code of 93-1 shows that the first printing of the book occurred in 1993.

Printed in the United States of America

Screen reproductions for this book were created by means of the program Collage Plus from Inner Media, Inc., Hollis, NH.

Publisher: *Marie Butler-Knight*
Managing Editor: *Liz Keaffaber*
Product Development Manager: *Faith Wempen*
Acquisitions Manager: *Barry Pruett*
Development Editor: *Mary Cole Rack*
Production Editor: *Linda Hawkins*
Manuscript Editor: *Barry Childs-Helton*
Cover Design: *Jay Corpus*
Designer: *Barbara Webster*
Indexer: *C. Small*
Production Team: *Gary Adair, Diana Bigham-Griffin, Katy Bodenmiller, Brad Chinn, Kim Cofer, Meshell Dinn, Mark Enochs, Stephanie Gregory, Jenny Kucera, Beth Rago, Marc Shecter, Greg Simsic*

Special thanks to C. Herbert Feltner for ensuring the technical accuracy of this book.

Contents

Introduction xi
Add-Ins—Making Add-Ins Available 1
Audit—Tracing Dependents 3
Audit—Tracing Precedents 4
AutoFill—Copying a Cell's Contents 5
AutoFill—Copying a Cell's Format 6
AutoFilter 7
AutoFormat 7
AutoSum 7

Cells—Adding Borders 8
Cells—Aligning Data 10
Cells—AutoFill 12
Cells—Changing the Appearance of Text 12
Cells—Changing the Appearance of Numbers 14
Cells—Clearing 15
Cells—Copying 17
Cells—Copying the Format of 17
Cells—Deleting 18
Cells—Editing Labels, Values, and Dates 19
Cells—Entering Labels, Values, and Dates 19
Cells—Go To 20
Cells—Hiding 21
Cells—Inserting 21
Cells—Moving Data 23
Cells—Naming 23
Cells—Protecting 23
Cells—Selecting 24
Cells—Showing the Active Cell 24
Chart—Activating 24
Chart—Adding Data 25
Chart—Arrows 26
Chart—AutoFormat 26
Chart—Axes Labels 27

Chart—Calculate Now 27
Chart—Chart Type 28
Chart—Creating an Embedded Chart 29
Chart—Creating in a Separate Document 30
Chart—Data Labels 31
Chart—Deleting Data 32
Chart—Drawing Objects on 33
Chart—Editing a Series 33
Chart—Error Bars 34
Chart—Exploding a Pie Piece 34
Chart—Formatting a 3-D View 35
Chart—Formatting 36
Chart—Formatting Numbers 38
Chart—Formatting Text 38
Chart—Gallery 39
Chart—Gridlines 40
Chart—Legend 40
Chart—Lines and Bars 41
Chart—Moving 42
Chart—Resizing 43
Chart—Moving a Chart Object 43
Chart—Printing 43
Chart—Protecting 44
Chart—Scaling 44
Chart—Selecting 45
Chart—Sizing 46
Chart—Spell Checking 47
Chart—Text 47
Chart—Titles 48
Chart—Trendlines 48
Chart—Unprotecting 49
Column—Changing Width 50
Column—Deleting 51
Column—Inserting 51
Column—Hiding 51
Column—Selecting 51

Data—Aligning in a Cell 52
Data—Changing the Appearance of 52

Data—Clearing 52
Data—Copying...52
Data—Copying the Format of..............................54
Data—Cutting and Pasting 55
Data—Deleting 56
Data—Editing in a Cell 57
Data—Entering Labels, Values, and Dates.............58
Data—Finding..59
Data—Inserting Copied or Cut Cells....................61
Data—Moving 61
Data—Pasting...62
Data—Paste Special 63
Data—Replacing 65
Data—Protecting..67
Data—Styles 67
Data List—Adding a Record 67
Data List—Analyzing Data 68
Data List—Creating...68
Data List—Data Form 69
Data List—Deleting a Record...............................70
Data List—Editing a Record 71
Data List—Filtering with Advanced Filter 72
Data List—Filtering with AutoFilter 75
Data List—Finding a Record 76
Data List—Sorting a List 78
Data List—Subtotals..80
Database..82
Database—Extracting Data 82
Display Options—Changing 83
Drawing Tools 83

Editing Cell Entries 83
Editing Database Records 83
Embedded Objects—Creating 83
Embedded Objects—Editing 85
Exiting 85

File—Closing 86
File—Finding 86

File—New 88
File—Opening 88
File—Saving 88
File—Saving a Copy of 88
Find and Replace 88
Format Painter 88
Formatting—Cells and Data 88
Formula—Absolute and
Relative References 89
Formula—Adding Numbers..........................90
Formula—Creating 90
Formula—Entering 3-D References 92
Formula—Entering Linking References 94
Formula—Functions 95
Formula—Goal Seeking................................96
Formula—Protecting 97
Formula—Setting
Calculation Options 97
Formula—Scenarios 99
Formula—Solver 100
Formula—Totals 102
Formula—Using Named Cells and Ranges 103
Formula—Viewing in Cells 104
Functions—Inserting with
the Function Wizard 104

Go To 106
Graphic Objects—Bringing to Front 106
Graphic Objects—Copying 107
Graphic Objects—Creating 107
Graphic Objects—Deleting 109
Graphic Objects—Drawing Toolbar 109
Graphic Objects—Formatting.....................109
Graphic Objects—Grouping
and Ungrouping 111
Graphic Objects—Inserting Pictures 112
Graphic Objects—Moving 112
Graphic Objects—Selecting 113
Graphic Objects—Sending to Back 114

Graphic Objects—Sizing and Shaping 114

Help—Getting Help 115
Help—TipWizard 116

Links—Creating 117
Links—Updating 118

Macro—Adding to a Button 120
Macro—Adding to a Toolbar 121
Macro—Adding to the Tools Menu 122
Macro—Pausing Recording 123
Macro—Recording 124
Macro—Resuming Recording 127
Macro—Running 128
Margins—Changing 129
Menu Commands—Selecting 129
Microsoft Query—Creating a Data Source 130
Microsoft Query—Creating a Query 132
Microsoft Query—Selecting Specific Records
  to Extract 135

Names—Applying Cell and Range Names 137
Names—Creating From Labels 138
Names—Defining Cell and Range Names 139
New File 140
New Workbook 140
Number—Formatting 140

OLE (Object Linking and Embedding) 141
Open File 141
Open Workbook 141
Orientation 141
Outline—Creating 141
Outline—Displaying and Hiding Detail 142
Outline—Removing 143

Page Breaks—Automatic 143
Page Breaks—Inserting and Removing 143

Page Setup—Headers and Footers 144
Page Setup—Margins 145
Page Setup—Page Size and Orientation 147
Page Setup—Sheet Preferences 148
Page Size—Setting 150
Pictures—Inserting 150
Preview Printing 150
Pivot Table—Creating from a Data List 150
Pivot Table—Rearranging 152
Printing—Print Area 153
Printing—Print Preview 153
Printing—Print Titles 155
Printing—Workbook 155
Printing—Worksheet 157

Range—Applying Names 157
Range—Defining Names 157
Range—Filling Cells 157
Range—Filling with Series 158
Range—Selecting 159
Repeating—Operations and Commands 159
Row—Changing Height 160
Row—Deleting 161
Row—Hiding 161
Row—Inserting 162
Row—Selecting 162

Save—Workbook, Chart, Slideshow 162
Scenarios—Creating 163
Scenarios—Viewing 164
Selecting Cells, Columns, and Rows 165
Selecting Columns 166
Selecting Multiple Ranges of Cells 166
Selecting Rows 167
Selecting Worksheets 167
Series—Creating an AutoFill Series 168
Series—Filling Cells with Related Values 169
Shortcut Menu 172
Slide Show—Creating 172

Spelling—Checking 174
Starting Excel 176
Styles—Applying 176
Styles—Creating 177
Subtotals—Summarizing and Analyzing Data 178
Summarizing and Analyzing Data 178

TipWizard—Turning On and Off 178
Toolbars—Customizing 179
Toolbars—Selecting a Button 180
Toolbars—Showing and Hiding 180
Toolbars—Tear-Off Palettes 182
Toolbars—Button Descriptions 183
ToolTips 183

Undo—Commands and Operations 184

View—Changing the Show Options 184
View—Freezing Titles 187
View—Full Screen 188
View—Hiding Cells 188
View—Zoom 189
View Manager—Adding a View 191
View Manager—Switching Between Views 192

Window—Activating 193
Window—Arranging 193
Window—Closing 194
Window—Freezing 194
Window—Maximizing 195
Window—Minimizing 195
Window—Moving 196
Window—New Window 197
Window—Protecting 198
Window—Restoring 198
Window—Sizing 199
Window—Splitting 199
Window—Zooming 201

Workbook—Changing the Number of
Default Worksheets 201
Workbook—Closing 201
Workbook—New 201
Workbook—Opening 202
Workbook—Printing 204
Workbook—Protecting 204
Workbook—Saving 205
Workbook—Saving With a New Name 207
Worksheet—Copying 208
Worksheet—Deleting 210
Worksheet—Displaying Multiple Worksheets 210
Worksheet—Grouping 211
Worksheet—Hiding 211
Worksheet—Inserting 212
Worksheet—Moving 212
Worksheet—Moving Between 214
Worksheet—Moving Within 215
Worksheet—Naming 217
Worksheet—New 218
Worksheet—Printing 218
Worksheet—Protecting 218
Worksheet—Saving 220
Worksheet—Selecting 220
Worksheet—Selecting Multiple Worksheets 220
Workspace—Saving 220

Index 222

Introduction

With short and clear step-by-step instructions, the One Minute Reference Excel 5 *offers unique help when you are in a hurry. This book is designed for the person who:*

- Doesn't have time to flip through a large manual.

- Wants only the steps necessary to accomplish a task, and not a lot of text.

- Wants no-nonsense instructions to complete a task.

The *One Minute Reference Excel 5* gives easy-to-understand steps for the tasks you need to accomplish quickly.

Conventions Used in This Book

This book presents Excel in ways that will make using the program as simple as possible:

- **Alphabetical organization**   Tasks are in alphabetical order for instant fingertip access to important topics.

- **Keycap column**   All steps are concise. Listed to the right of each step, you will find the keys to press (or the information to type) to accomplish a task.

Keys to press are shown as *keycaps*
like this ....⏎

Information to type is shown
in bold italic text like this ....***text***

- **Optional steps**   Some steps begin
  with the word (**Optional**). You
  may skip those steps if you wish!

- **Key combinations**   Key combinations are often used to accomplish a task. For example, if you
  are asked to press **Alt**+**A**,
  press the **Alt** key and the **A**
  at the same time.

- **Selection letters**   Each menu and
  command has one bold letter in its
  name which you use when making
  keyboard selections. Menu and
  command names in this book
  show the selection letters in
  bold print.

- **Multiple options**   If you see "*or*"
  in a step, use the method of your
  choice for that step.

- **Some steps require more than
  one keypress or action**.

In that case, you'll see the actions listed
vertically, like this ....

This icon points out extra information
about Excel 5.0, or techniques many
people find valuable when using Excel's
features.

This icon identifies examples of how to
use the feature being discussed.

This icon points out quick steps for
accomplishing the same task with a mouse.

Excel 5.0 Basics

*Excel 5.0 is a spreadsheet program and more. You
can use Excel to analyze data, perform calculations, organize lists, prepare charts that summarize
complex relationships, and create "what-if" analy-
ses. Excel 5.0 makes it simple to manipulate large
amounts of data: in most cases, a click of the
mouse activates a command. But don't race to lay
out your first spreadsheet just yet! Before you can
take advantage of Excel, you must learn some
basics.*

Starting Excel 5.0

To start Excel 5.0, do the following:

1. At the DOS prompt, type .... **WIN**

2. Press .... ⬅

3. Double-click on the program group that contains the Excel 5.0 icon (usually the "Microsoft Office" program group).

4. Double-click on the **Microsoft Excel** icon.

5. Wait for the Excel 5.0 screen to appear.

If you have not installed Excel 5.0 on your computer, follow these steps to install it:

1. Put the Excel 5.0 Setup 1 disk in drive A or drive B.

2. Change to the Windows Program Manager.

3. Select the File menu .... F

4. Select **Run** .... R

5. Type **A:SETUP** (or **B:SETUP**).

6. Read on-screen instructions and follow prompts until a message appears, telling you installation is complete.

The Excel 5.0 title screen appears for a few moments, and then Excel 5.0 displays an empty *workbook* (collection of separate worksheets) you can begin using right away. Workbooks make it easy to organize complex data. For example, you could copy one week's expense report to five different *worksheets*, and have a month's expenses stored in one *workbook*.

Parts of an Excel 5.0 Screen

The Excel 5.0 contains several elements that are common to all Windows programs. Here's a brief summary:

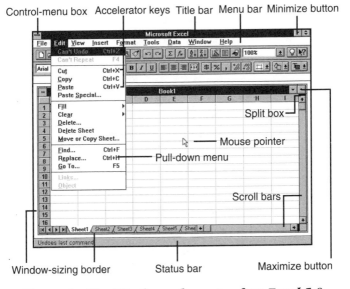

Figure 1   The Windows elements of an Excel 5.0 screen.

- **Menu bar** Located below the title bar, this bar contains the *pull-down menus* available in the program.

- **Accelerator keys** Often you will see keystroke letters and numbers to the right of a command name. You can use these keys to access a command directly, without having to open a menu first to select the command.

- **Control-menu box** In the upper left corner of a window or screen, this box looks like a square with a hyphen in it. When you click on it, a pull-down menu appears, offering size and location controls for the window.

- **Title bar** This bar across the top of a window or screen shows the name of the window, workbook, or program.

- **Minimize and Maximize buttons** Located at the upper right corner of a window or screen, these buttons look like up and down arrow points; they alter a window's size. The Minimize button shrinks the window to the size of an icon. The Maximize button expands the window to fill the screen. When maximized, a window contains a double-arrow *Restore* *button*, which returns the window to its previous size.

- **Split box** Double-click here to split one window in two; this lets you view and work in different areas of the same worksheet.

- **Status bar** Displays a description of a selected command or tool, the progress of a current operation, and whether certain keys (such as Num Lock and Caps Lock) are active.

- **Window-sizing border** Drag here to resize a window.

- **Mouse pointer** When you move the mouse, you control this on-screen pointer (usually an arrow as in the figure).

- **Scroll bars** Scroll bars appear at the bottom and right sides of a window when it contains too much information to display. Use the *scroll arrows* (at each end of a scroll bar) to move through the document slowly, or the *scroll box* (on the bar) to move quickly from one screen to the next.

Distinctive Excel 5.0 Elements

In addition to screen elements familiar to all Windows users, Excel 5.0 contains some unique features:

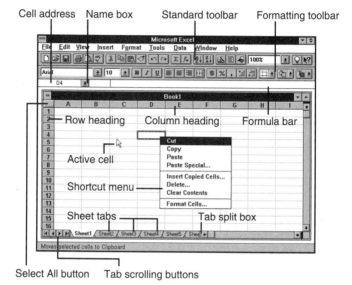

Figure 2   Elements unique to Excel 5.0.

- **Column heading**   Letters in gray-shaded boxes at the top of each column which help to identify it.

- **Row heading**   Numbers in gray-shaded boxes to the left of each row which help to identify it.

- **Standard toolbar** Contains buttons to activate the most commonly used commands, such as opening, saving, and printing a workbook. You may customize this toolbar, and all the others, to make your favorite commands accessible.

- **Formatting toolbar** Contains buttons for formatting the contents of cells. Additional toolbars can be displayed and positioned anywhere within the worksheet area.

- **Cell address** The combination of the column heading and row heading for a cell. For example, the cell in the second column, third row has a cell address of B3.

- **Formula bar** Displays the contents of a cell, and lets you make changes. The cell address appears in the *name box.*

- **Name box** A drop-down list box located on the formula bar; lists the worksheet's named cells and ranges.

- **Select All button** Click here to select all the cells in a worksheet.

- **Active cell**   Data you type appears in the active cell, distinguished by its darker outline.

- **Shortcut menu**   Click on the right mouse button anywhere in the window (during any operation) for a menu with commands specific to the current task.

- **Sheet tabs**   Tabs which identify the worksheets which make up a workbook. Click on a tab to bring that worksheet to the screen for you to view and work with. There are 16 worksheets in a workbook; you may delete some or add more.

- **Tab scrolling buttons**   Scroll through the worksheets of a workbook by clicking these buttons. The first button scrolls to the first worksheet, the last button scrolls to the last worksheet. The middle buttons move through the worksheets one at a time in the indicated direction.

- **Tab split box**   Drag this split box to control the size of tab area, or that of the horizontal scroll bar.

Using a Mouse

To work efficiently in Excel, you should use a mouse. You press the mouse buttons and slide the mouse along a flat surface (such as your computer table) to accomplish tasks quickly. Here are the basic actions you perform with the mouse:

- To *point* means to move the tip of the mouse pointer onto an item by moving the mouse.

- To *click on* an item means to press the mouse button once after moving the pointer onto an item. Unless otherwise instructed, always use the left mouse button.

- To *double-click on* an item means to click the mouse button twice quickly after moving the mouse pointer onto it.

- To *drag* means to move the mouse pointer onto an item, press and hold down the mouse button, and then slide the mouse along a flat surface. Release the mouse button only when you have placed the on-screen item where you want it.

Choosing Menus and Commands

*The menu bar contains the names of various pull-
down menus from which you can select commands.
All menu names, and the commands on each menu,
contain one underlined letter. These are called
selection letters, and they are printed in **bold** in
this book. You press the selection letter to choose a
menu or command with the keyboard when you
don't use a mouse. To open a menu and choose a
command, you can use either the mouse steps or the
keyboard steps described here:*

Mouse Steps

1. Click on the menu name on the menu bar.

2. Click on the desired command.

Keyboard Steps

1. Choose the menu ....`Alt`+*selection letter*

2. Choose the command.............*selection letter*

TIP

Notice that some commands are followed by
key names such as **Ctrl+O** (for the **O**pen **F**ile
command). These are called **accelerator
keys**. You can use these keys to perform the
command without even opening the menu.

Usually, when you select a command, the action is
performed immediately. However:

  • If the command name appears gray (rather
    than black), the command is unavailable at

the moment, and you cannot choose it until some prior action occurs.

- If the command name is followed by an arrow, selecting that command will open another menu, from which you select an option.

- If the command name is followed by an ellipsis (three dots), selecting it will cause a dialog box to appear. You'll learn about dialog boxes in the next section.

Using the Toolbars, Shortcut Menus, and Wizards

Excel 5.0 provides several **toolbars**, *containing* **buttons** *(tools) related to specific activities such as formatting a cell's contents, customizing a chart, querying and/or analyzing data, and adding drawn objects such as arrows. You activate the buttons by clicking on them. If you have the toolbar for your current activity displayed on the screen, you can quickly perform related commands.*

Shortcut menus *are pop-up groups of commands which are opened by clicking the* **right** *mouse button in different areas of the screen. They offer short-cuts to some of the choices on toolbars and menus. Click the right mouse button and Excel provides the shortcut menu that relates to your current activity.*

Wizards guide you step-by-step through various processes. For example, you can use a Wizard to create an Excel chart, enter formulas, import text, or create a pivot table—right away.

Navigating Dialog Boxes

A **dialog box** is Windows' way of requesting additional information. To open a dialog box, choose a command from one of the menus on the menu bar. Each dialog box contains one or more of the following elements:

- *List boxes* display available choices. To activate a list, click inside the list box. You can also press **Tab** to move from option to option. If the entire list is not visible, use the scroll bar to view the items in the list. To select an item from the list, click on it.

- *Drop-down lists* are similar to list boxes, but only one item in the list is shown at first. To see the rest of the items, click on the **down arrow** in the right corner of the box. To select an item from the list, click on it.

- *Text boxes* allow you to type entries. To activate a text box, click inside it. To edit an existing entry, use the **arrow** keys to move the cursor, and the **Delete** or **Backspace** keys to delete existing characters. Then type your correction.

- *Check boxes* allow you to select one or more items in a group of options. For example, if you are styling text or numbers, you may select Bold and Italic to have the data appear in both bold and italic type. Click on a check box to activate it. To deactivate the command, clear the check box by clicking on it again.

- *Option buttons* are like check boxes, but you can select only one option button in a group. Selecting one button deselects any option already selected. Click on an option button to activate it.

- *Command buttons* execute (or cancel) the command once you have made your selection in the dialog box. To select a command button, click on it.

To close a dialog box, make your decisions and click on **OK**, or on **Cancel** to discontinue the activity.

Navigating Between Worksheets

*To switch between worksheets in a workbook, click on the appropriate tab. If the tab is not displayed, use the **Tab Scrolling** buttons to move between worksheets in the indicated direction. To move to the first worksheet in a workbook, click on the first Tab Scrolling button. To move to the last worksheet, click on the last button.*

Selecting and Deselecting Cells

Whenever you work with Excel, you will use these techniques to define the portion of the worksheet you want to edit, copy, move, delete, or enhance. Cells are selected in rectangular blocks called **ranges**. *The cells you select will be highlighted.*

Mouse Steps

Here are several ways to use the mouse to select cells in Excel:

- To select a range of cells, click in the upper left-hand cell, and drag to the lower right-hand cell.

- To select an entire row or column, click on the row or column heading. To select more than one row or column, just drag the mouse pointer over the appropriate headings.

- To select all the cells in a worksheet, click on the **Select All** button.

- To select non-adjacent cells or ranges, hold the **Ctrl** key down as you move the mouse to the additional cells, and drag to select them.

TIP

To deselect cells, click the mouse button outside the selected range.

Keyboard Steps

*Use the **arrow** keys to position the cursor at the beginning of the cell range you want to select. Press and hold the **Shift** key, and use the **arrow** keys to select a range of cells.*

To select	*Press*
One cell to the right	Shift + →
One cell to the left	Shift + ←
The line above	Shift + ↑
The line below	Shift + ↓
Entire row	Shift + Space
Entire column	Ctrl + Space
Entire worksheet	Ctrl + Shift + Space
Current data region	Ctrl + Shift + *
Extend selection to the edge of the data region	Ctrl + Shift + ← → ↑ ↓

To deselect cells, press ⬆, ⬇, ➡, or ⬅.

TIP

Exiting Excel 5.0

When you are ready to exit the program, click on the File menu, and then click on the Exit command. Excel will ask if you want to save your work; if you answer Yes, Excel will provide some options for you to choose. After you make your choices, you will be returned safely to Windows.

Add-Ins—Making Add-Ins Available

Allows you to make additional Excel features available. If you performed a complete installation of Excel, you can make the following add-ins available:

Add-in	What It Does
Analysis ToolPak	Adds financial and engineering functions, and tools for performing statistical and engineering analysis.
AutoSave	Saves workbooks automatically as you work.
Microsoft ODBC Support	Adds functions that let you retrieve data from outside sources using Microsoft Open Database Connectivity (ODBC).
Microsoft Query Add-in	Lets you retrieve and combine data from two or more database files, including Paradox, dBase, and FoxPro files.
Report Manager	Allows you to create and print reports consisting of views and scenarios.

Slide Show	Lets you create a slide show using worksheets and charts.
Solver	Lets you play what-if with your worksheet data.
View Manager	Saves a window as a view, and allows you to apply saved views to different worksheets to see the data as it would appear in different formats.

EXAMPLE

If you turn on the Microsoft Query add-in, the Data menu will contain the command Get External Data. Selecting this command runs Microsoft Query, a program that allows you to get data from one or more database files and insert that data into an Excel worksheet.

1. Open the Tools menu ....⎡Alt⎤+⎡T⎤

2. Choose Add-Ins ....⎡I⎤

3. Click on the add-in you want to make available (this puts an X in its check box).

4. Select **OK**.

TIP

If the add-in you want is not on the list, click on the **B**rowse button, and use the Browse dialog box to locate the add-in file (these files have the extensions **.XLL** and **.XLA**). The add-in files are usually in the \EXCEL\LIBRARY directory or one of its subdirectories:
\EXCEL\LIBRARY\ANALYSIS,
\EXCEL\LIBRARY\MSQUERY,
\EXCEL\LIBRARY\SLIDES, or
\EXCEL\LIBRARY\SOLVER.

Audit—Tracing Dependents

*Uses arrows to connect the current cell to any other cell that contains a formula which depends on the current cell's contents. To trace **precedent cells** (cells upon which the contents of the current cell depend), see "Audit—Tracing Precedents."*

EXAMPLE

Use this command to correct errors caused by incorrect cell references in formulas.

TIP

To remove the displayed arrows, click on the **Remove All Arrows** button on the **Auditing** toolbar, or select the Tools Auditing Remove All Arrows command.

1. Move to the cell whose dependents you wish to trace .... ⬆ ⬇ ⬅ ➡

2. Open the Tools menu .... Alt + T

3. Select the Auditing submenu ....

4. Select Trace Dependents .... **D**

MOUSE

Instead of steps 2 to 4, click on the **Trace Dependents** button on the **Auditing** toolbar.

Audit—Tracing Precedents

*Uses arrows to connect the current cell to any other cell upon which the contents of the current cell depend. To trace **dependent cells** (cells containing a formula which depends on the contents of the current cell), see "Audit—Tracing Dependents."*

TIP

Use this command to correct errors in formulas that were caused by incorrect cell references.

TIP

To remove the displayed arrows, click on the **Remove All Arrows** button on the **Auditing** toolbar, or select the Tools Auditing Remove All Arrows command.

1. Move to the cell whose precedents you wish to trace ...... **↑** **↓** **←** **→**

2. Open the Tools menu .... **Alt** + **T**

3. Select the Auditing submenu ....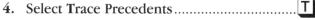

4. Select Trace Precedents .... T

MOUSE

Instead of steps 2 to 4, click on the **Trace Precedents** button on the **Auditing** toolbar.

AutoFill—Copying a Cell's Contents

*Copies data to adjacent cells by dragging the **fill handle**, a small square located at the bottom right-hand edge of a selected cell or range. You can also use this command to fill a range of cells automatically with related values—for example, you could fill a row of column headings with sequential months: January, February, March, etc. See "Series—Creating an AutoFill Series." To copy the format of a cell instead of its value, see "AutoFill—Copying a Cell's Format."*

You can use a similar command to fill a range of cells automatically with related values—such as January, February, March, etc. See "Series—Filling Cells With Related Values." To copy the format of a cell instead of its value, see "AutoFill—Copying a Cell's Format."

Mouse Steps

1. Select the cell whose value you wish to copy.

2. Select the fill handle.

3. Drag the fill handle down, or to the right; this selects the cells to which to copy the value.

4. Release the mouse button.

Keyboard Steps

1. Move to the cell whose value you wish to copy .... ↑ ↓ ← →

2. Select the range to which you want to copy the selected value .... **Shift** + ↑ ↓ ← →

3. Open the Edit menu .... **Alt** + **E**

4. Select Fill .... **I**

5. Select either **D**own or **R**ight .... **D** or **R**

TIP

Instead of steps 3 to 5, press **Ctrl+D** to fill down, or **Ctrl+R** to fill right.

AutoFill—Copying a Cell's Format

Copies a cell's format to adjacent cells. To copy the cell's value instead, see "AutoFill—Copying a Cell's Value."

1. Select the cell whose format you wish to copy.

2. Using the right mouse button, select the **fill handle**.

3. Drag the fill handle down, or to the right; this selects the cells to which to copy the formats.

4. Release the right mouse button.

5. Select **Fill Formats** from the shortcut menu.

AutoFilter

See "Data List—Filtering With AutoFilter."

AutoFormat

Automatically formats a table.

1. Place the cursor within the table you want to format.

2. Open the Format menu .... Alt +O

3. Select AutoFormat .... A

4. Select a format from the list .... ↑ ↓

5. Select **OK** .... ↵

AutoSum

Totals cells immediately above or to the left.

1. Select a cell below or to the right of a group of cells whose values you want to total.

TIP

You can create totals in multiple cells at one time. To do so, select several blank cells adjacent to the columns or rows whose values you want to total. For example, select cells **A3..C3** to total the values in rows 1 and 2, columns A, B, and C. You can also select a range of values, and the appropriate blank cells, to create both column and row totals at the same time.

2. Click on the **AutoSum** button on the **Standard** toolbar.

Cells—Adding Borders

Adds a border and shading around selected cells.

1. Select the cells you want to surround with a border.

TIP

To select the entire worksheet to surround with a border, click on the **Select All** button or press **Ctrl+Shift+Spacebar**.

2. Open the Format menu .... **Alt** + **O**
3. Select Cells .... **E**

TIP

Instead of steps 2 and 3, press **Ctrl+1**.

Instead of steps 2 and 3, select **Format Cells** from the shortcut menu.

MOUSE

4. Select the **Border** tab .... Ctrl + Tab

5. Select any of the following options:

   Outline .... Alt + O

   Left .... Alt + L

   Right .... Alt + R

   Top .... Alt + T

   Bottom .... Alt + B

   Style .... Alt + E

   ↑ ↓ ← →

   Color .... Alt + C

   ↑ ↓ ← →

6. When finished adding a border,
   press .... ↵

You can add the most popular border styles through the **Borders** drop-down list button on the **Formatting** toolbar.

MOUSE

Cells—Aligning Data

Aligns the data within selected cells. The following options are found under the Alignment tab in the Format Cells dialog box.

Options	Description
Horizontal	
General	Left-aligns text and right-aligns numbers (this is the default alignment).
Left	Left-aligns data.
Center	Centers data.
Right	Right-aligns data.
Fill	Repeats a character to fill a cell.
Justify	Aligns text to the right and left borders of a cell.
Center across	Centers data across a range of selected cells.
Vertical	
Top	Aligns data at the cell's top border.
Center	Aligns data vertically at the cell's center.

Bottom	Aligns data at the bottom border of the cell.
Justify	Aligns text between the top and bottom borders of a cell.
Orientation	Selects an orientation style.
Wrap Text	Wraps text to another line in a cell if the data is too long.

1. Select the cells you want to align.

2. Open the Format menu ....[Alt]+[O]

3. Select Cells ....[E]

TIP

Instead of steps 2 and 3, press **Ctrl+1**.

MOUSE

Instead of steps 2 and 3, select **Format Cells** from the shortcut menu.

4. Select the **Alignment** tab ....[Ctrl]+[Tab]

5. Select any alignment option from the preceding table by pressing...............[Alt]+

selection letter

6. When finished selecting an
    alignment option, press ....

MOUSE
You can left-, right-, or center-align the
data in cells quickly with the Center Across
Columns, Align Left, Align Right, and
Center buttons on the **Formatting**
toolbar.

Cells—AutoFill

*See "AutoFill—Copying a Cell's Value," "AutoFill—
Copying a Cell's Format," and "Series—Filling Cells
With Related Values."*

Cells—Changing the Appearance of Text

*Changes the font, style, size, effects, and color on
selected data in a cell, range, or an entire document.*

1. Select the cells, range, or document
    whose format you want to change.

2. Open the Format menu ....[Alt]+[O]

3. Select Cells ....[E]

TIP
Instead of steps 2 and 3, press **Ctrl+1**.

MOUSE

Instead of steps 2 and 3, select **Format Cells** from the shortcut menu.

4. Select the **Font** tab ....`Ctrl`+`Tab`

5. Select any of the following
   options to change:

   Font ....`Alt`+`F`

   Font Style ....`Alt`+`O`

   Size ....`Alt`+`S`

   Color ....`Alt`+`C`

   Underline ....`Alt`+`U`

   Strikethrough ....`Alt`+`K`

   Superscript ....`Alt`+`E`

   Subscript ....`Alt`+`B`

TIP

To reset the font, select Normal Font by pressing **Alt+N** from the **Font** tab.

6. To save the settings, press ....`⏎`

TIP

Instead of following the steps listed here, select the cells, and press these keys:

Bold	Ctrl+B
Italic	Ctrl+I
Underline	Ctrl+U
Strikethrough	Ctrl+5

MOUSE

You can quickly format text with the Font, Font Size, Bold, Italic, Underline, and Font Color buttons on the **Formatting** toolbar.

Cells—Changing the Appearance of Numbers

Changes the format of numbers in a cell, range, or an entire document.

1. Select the cells, range, or document whose format you want to change.

2. Open the Format menu .... Alt + O

3. Select Cells .... E

TIP

Instead of steps 2 and 3, press **Ctrl+1**.

MOUSE

Instead of steps 2 and 3, select **Format Cells** from the shortcut menu.

4. Select the **Number** tab .... Ctrl + Tab

5. Select a **Category** .... Alt + C
                                     ↑ ↓

6. Select from the **Format Codes** .... Alt + F
                                     ↑ ↓

7. To save the settings, press ....

TIP

Instead of following the steps listed here, select the cells, and press these keys:

General	Ctrl+Shift+~
0.00	Ctrl+Shift+!
h:mm	Ctrl+Shift+@
d-mmm-yy	Ctrl+Shift+#
$#,##0.00	Ctrl+Shift+$
0%	Ctrl+Shift+%
0.00E+00	Ctrl+Shift+ ^

MOUSE

You can quickly format numbers with the Currency Style, Percent Style, Comma Style, Increase Decimals, and Decrease Decimals buttons on the Formatting toolbar.

Cells—Clearing

Removes the contents of a selected cell or range of cells (including values, text, data, formulas, notes, and formats).

TIP

There's a difference between the **Edit Clear** and **Edit Delete** commands. **Edit Clear** simply clears the contents (data and/or formatting) in a cell. **Edit Delete** deletes the contents plus the cell itself, shifting the surrounding cells to fill the space vacated by the deleted cell.

Mouse Steps

These steps clear the contents of a cell only. To clear the format, notes, or the entire cell, follow the keyboard steps.

1. Select the cell(s) to clear.

2. Click on the **fill handle**.

3. Drag *up or to the left*, into the selection. (The selected cells will turn gray.)

4. Release the mouse button.

MOUSE In place of steps 2 and 3, you can click the right mouse button to bring up the shortcut menu, and select **Clear Contents**.

MOUSE To clear both the contents and the format of a cell, press and hold **Ctrl** while dragging the fill handle into the selection.

Keyboard Steps

1. Select the cell(s) to clear .... **Shift** + ↑ ↓ ← →

2. Open the Edit menu .... **Alt** + **E**

3. Select Clear .... **A**

TIP You can also press the **Del** key to clear the contents of a cell.

4. Select any of the following Clear
   options:

   All .... A

   Formats .... F

   Contents C

   Notes .... N

Cells—Copying

See "Data—Copying."

Cells—Copying the Format of

Copies the format of the selected data and cells and pastes the format onto another selected range of cells.

1. Click on the cell whose formatting you want to copy.

2. Click on the **Format Painter** button in the **Standard** toolbar (the button with the paintbrush on it).

3. Select the cell(s) to which you want to copy the format.

4. Release the mouse button.

TIP

You can also copy the format by using the Copy and Paste Special commands on the Edit menu. Select the cell whose format you want to copy, and select **Edit/Copy**. Select the cell(s) you want to copy the format to, and choose **Edit/Paste Special**. When the dialog box appears, click on Formats, and click on **OK**.

Cells—Deleting

Deletes a selected cell, row, or column (including data, formulas, and formatting) from the active worksheet. The cells surrounding the deletion will shift to fill the empty space.

TIP

There may be confusion between the Edit Clear and Edit Delete command. Edit Clear simply removes the contents of a cell. Edit Delete removes the cell itself, shifting cells to eliminate the space left by deleting a cell.

1. Select the cell, row, or
   column to delete .... Shift + ↑ ↓ ← →

TIP

To select an entire row or column, click on the row or column head.

2. Open the Edit menu .... Alt + E
3. Select Delete .... D

MOUSE

Instead of steps 2 and 3, click the right mouse button and select **Delete** from the shortcut menu.

TIP

You can also press **Ctrl+- (minus sign)** to delete selected cells, rows, or columns.

4. Select any of the following options from the **Delete** dialog box:

Shift Cells **L**eft .... Alt + L

Shift Cells **U**p .... Alt + U

Entire **R**ow .... Alt + R

Entire **C**olumn .... Alt + C

5. Press .... ⏎

Cells—Editing Labels, Values, and Dates

See "Data—Editing in a Cell."

Cells—Entering Labels, Values, and Dates

See "Data—Entering Labels, Values and Dates."

Cells—Go To

Moves the cursor directly to the cell, range of cells, or named range you specify. To search for specific text within a worksheet, see "Data—Finding." For information on moving within a worksheet or between worksheets, see "Worksheet—Moving Between" and "Worksheet—Moving Within."

EXAMPLE

You can use this command with large worksheets when you don't want to use the scroll keys to look for your selection. You can jump across large numbers of cells. For example, if you are presently in cell C10 and want to go to a cell several screens away (like AZ355), you can use the Go To command.

1. Open the Edit menu .... `Alt`+`E`
2. Select Go To .... `G`

TIP

Instead of steps 1 and 2, press **F5**.

3. In the Reference box, enter a cell's address, range, or range name to go to .... `Alt`+`R`
    address

EXAMPLE

You can go to any cell or range in a workbook by referencing the sheet name, followed by an exclamation point, followed by a cell or range address, as in SALESHT!QTR4_TOTAL.

MOUSE

You can go directly to a named cell or range by selecting it from the **Name** box on the formula bar.

4. When ready to go to the cell(s),

   press .... ↵

Cells—Hiding

See "View—Hiding Cells."

Cells—Inserting

Inserts a blank cell, range, row, or column into the active worksheet. The inserted blank cells appear in whatever location and shape you select. Inserting will shift the cells surrounding the insertion to make room. To copy cells and insert them into the worksheet at another location, see "Data—Inserting Copied or Cut Cells."

Mouse Steps

1. Select the blank cell(s), range, row, or column you want to insert.

MOUSE

To select an entire blank row or column, click on the row or column head.

2. Press and hold .... Shift

3. Drag the fill handle down or to the right, away from the selection, over the number of cells you want to insert.

4. Release the mouse button.

Keyboard Steps

1. Select a cell, blank range, row, or column to insert .... Shift + ↑ ↓ ← →

2. Open the Insert menu .... Alt + I

3. Select Cells .... E

TIP

You can also press **Ctrl+ + (plus sign)** to display the dialog box that lets you insert selected cells, rows, or columns.

4. Select any of the following options from the Insert dialog box:

Shift Cells Right .... Alt + I

Shift Cells Down .... Alt + D

Entire Row .... Alt + R

      Entire Column .... Alt + C

5. Press .... ↵

Cells—Moving Data

See "Data—Cutting and Pasting."

Cells—Naming

See "Ranges—Naming," and "Formula—Using Named Cells and Ranges."

Cells—Protecting

Prevents unauthorized changes to the contents of individual cells by protecting the worksheet. After locking cells, see "Worksheet—Protecting" or "Work-book—Protecting" for instructions on turning protection on.

1. Select the cells, range, or document whose contents you want to protect.

2. Open the Format menu .... Alt + O

3. Select Cells .... E

TIP

Instead of steps 2 and 3, press **Ctrl+1**.

MOUSE

Instead of steps 2 and 3, select **Format Cells** from the shortcut menu.

4. Select the **Protection** tab ....`Alt`+`Tab`

5. Select Locked ....`Alt`+`L`

6. To save the settings, press ....`↵`

Cells—Selecting

See "Selecting—Cells and Ranges."

Cells—Showing the Active Cell

Searches the worksheet to find and display the active cell.

1. Press ....`Ctrl`+`Back`

Chart—Activating

Makes the selected chart active so you can edit, format, and add arrows, text, colors, etc.

• To activate an embedded chart, double-click anywhere on the chart.

• To activate a chart which has been saved in its own window, open the
File menu...`Alt`+`F`
Select **Open** ....`O`
Type the chart file name ....*filename.ext*
Click on **OK** or press ....`↵`

Chart—Adding Data

Adds data to an existing chart. To delete data from a chart, see "Chart—Deleting Data." To change existing chart data, see "Chart—Editing Series."

1. Select the rows or columns of data to add.

2. Drag the selection to a chart.

TIP

If a chart is saved in a separate chart sheet (and not embedded into the worksheet) you will need to use the Copy and Paste Special commands on the Edit menu to add data instead of dragging.

MOUSE

You can also use this command to add axis labels to an existing chart. Simply select the labels, then drag them to the chart.

3. **(Optional)** If the **Paste Special** dialog box appears, select appropriate options:

    Add Cells as New **Series**—Add a new series.

    Add Cells as New **Point(s)**—Add data to existing series.

    Values (Y) in **R**ows—New data is organized in rows.

    Values (Y) in **C**olumns—New data is organized in columns.

Series **N**ames in First Row (Column)—Series names are in the first cell of each row or column of the new data.

Categories (X labels) in First Column (Row)— Labels are in the first cell of each row or column of the new data.

Replace Existing Categories—Replace existing data with new data.

4. **(Optional)** When you are through with the Paste Special dialog box, select **OK**.

Chart—Arrows

Adds an arrow to a chart to emphasize an impor- tant data point or series. See "Graphic Objects—Creating."

Chart—AutoFormat

Automatically formats a chart to a specific type and subtype. To change the chart type without affecting existing formatting, see "Chart—Chart Type." To further customize the chart after using AutoFormat, see "Chart—Formatting."

1. Activate the chart.

2. Open the Format menu.

3. Select the **A**utoFormat command.

MOUSE

Instead of steps 2 and 3, select the
AutoFormat command from the shortcut
menu.

4. Choose a chart type under **G**alleries.

5. Choose a subtype under **F**ormats.

6. Click on **OK**.

Chart—Axes Labels

*Displays or hides the X- and Y-axis labels and
markers. Axes labels are the text along the X and Y
axes that describe the chart data. To change the
scaling on an axis, see "Chart—Scaling."*

1. Activate the chart.

2. Open the Insert menu.

3. Select Axes.

4. Select the axes to display or hide. Clearing the
   check box hides the axes.

5. Select **OK**.

Chart—Calculate Now

*Recalculates the formulas in all open worksheets
and updates the corresponding charts. You need to
perform this operation only if you have set your
formulas to calculate manually (see "Formula—
Setting Calculation Options").*

1. Press F9

Chart—Chart Type

Changes the chart type of the entire chart, or just a data group, without affecting existing formatting. To format a chart automatically, see "Chart— AutoFormat." To customize the format of a chart, see "Chart—Formatting."

1. Activate the chart.

2. Open the Format menu.

3. Select Chart Type.

MOUSE

Instead of steps 2 and 3, select **Chart Type** from the shortcut menu.

4. **(Optional)** If there is more than one data group in the chart, select a data group from the **G**roup list.

5. **(Optional)** Choose between **2-D** and **3-D** chart dimensions.

6. Choose a chart type from those displayed.

MOUSE

Change a chart type quickly through the **Chart Type** drop-down list box on the **Chart** toolbar.

7. Click on **OK**.

TIP

To change the subtype, click on **Options** and select the **Subtype** tab. Choose a subtype and click on **OK**, or click on Chart Type to return to the Chart Type dialog box.

Chart—Creating an Embedded Chart

Creates an embedded chart step-by-step using the ChartWizard. To create a chart that's stored in its own file, see "Chart—Creating in Separate Document."

EXAMPLE

An *embedded chart* is placed within a worksheet, and not in its own file. Use an embedded chart to emphasize the relationship between a chart and its worksheet data.

TIP

You can change an existing chart with ChartWizard by activating the chart and repeating steps 4 to 10.

1. Select the range of cells containing the data you want to chart.

MOUSE

To select non-contiguous ranges, press **Ctrl** as you drag.

2. Click on the **ChartWizard** tool on the **Standard** toolbar.

3. Drag to select an area on the worksheet where the completed chart should be placed.

4. Verify the selected data range, then click on **Next**.

5. Select a chart type, then click on **Next**.

6. Select a chart format, then click on **Next**.

7. **(Optional)** Select applicable layout options.

8. Click on **Next**.

9. **(Optional)** Select applicable text options.

10. Click on **Finish**.

Chart—Creating in a Separate Document

Creates a chart in a separate document called a chart sheet, with or without the ChartWizard. To create an embedded chart (one that's part of the worksheet), see "Chart—Creating an Embedded Chart."

EXAMPLE

If you save a chart on its own chart sheet, it will be easier for you (and others) to locate within a workbook. By default, the chart sheet is named **Chart1**.

1. Select the range of cells which contain the data you want to chart.

MOUSE

To select non-contiguous ranges, press
Ctrl as you drag.

2. Open the Insert menu.

3. Select C**hart**.

4. Select **As** New Sheet.

TIP

To create a chart quickly in a separate
document (with the last selected chart
format), select the chart data and press
F11 or **Alt+F1**. This bypasses
ChartWizard.

5. Verify the selected data range, then click on
Next.

6. Select a chart type, then click on **Next**.

7. Select a chart format, then click on **Next**.

8. **(Optional)** Select applicable layout options.

9. Click on **Next**.

10. **(Optional)** Select applicable text options.

11. Click on **Finish**.

Chart—Data Labels

Adds data labels to active chart.

EXAMPLE

Data labels are used within the plot area to help identify each data marker. For example, in a column chart, use data labels to mark the *value* (relative height) of each column. You could also use data labels to identify what each column stands for by displaying its *label*.

1. Activate the chart.

2. Open the Insert menu.

3. Select **D**ata Labels.

MOUSE

Instead of steps 1 to 3, select **Insert Data Labels** from the shortcut menu.

4. Select a data label option.

5. **(Optional)** Select Show Legend **K**ey Next to Label.

6. Select **OK**.

Chart—Deleting Data

Deletes a data series from an existing chart, but does not delete data from the worksheet. To delete a chart object (such as a legend), see "Graphic Objects—Deleting."

1. Activate the chart.

2. Select the data series to delete.

For example, select one line in a line chart.

3. Open the **Edit** menu.

4. Select Cle**a**r.

5. Select **S**eries.

Instead of steps 3 to 5, simply press **Delete**.

Chart—Drawing Objects on

Adds arrows, text boxes, and other objects to a chart. See "Graphics Objects—Creating."

Chart—Editing a Series

Edits a data series in the active chart by changing its plot order. To change data series values, change them within their respective worksheet cells, and if necessary, recalculate the worksheet. See "Chart—Calculate Now." To add a new data series, see "Chart—Adding Data."

1. Activate the chart.

2. Click on the **ChartWizard** button on the **Chart** toolbar.

3. Click on **Next**.

4. Select the appropriate plot order: columns or rows.

5. Select **OK**.

Chart—Error Bars

Graphically depicts the margin of error inherent in the chart data.

1. Select the series to which you want to add error bars.

2. Open the **Insert** menu.

3. Select Error **Bars**.

MOUSE

Instead of steps 1 to 3, simply double-click on the series to which you want to add error bars, then select the **Y Error Bars** tab.

4. Select a **Display** type.

5. Select an error method and an error amount.

6. Click on **OK**.

Chart—Exploding a Pie Piece

"Explodes" (places at a distance) a piece of a pie chart, in order to emphasize it.

EXAMPLE

For example, explode the piece of a pie chart that represents a sales division, or a new product that has done exceptionally well.

1. Click on the pie piece to select it.

2. Drag it away from the rest of the chart. To replace an exploded piece, simply drag it back into place.

TIP

You can also use this command on a doughnut chart, to explode the pieces on the outer ring.

Chart—Formatting a 3-D View

Formats the angle in which the 3-D chart is viewed.

1. Activate the chart.

2. Open the Format menu.

3. Select 3-D View.

MOUSE

Instead of steps 2 and 3, select **3-D View** from the shortcut menu.

4. Make any necessary changes to the **E**levation, **R**otation, **P**erspective, and **H**eight.

5. **(Optional)** Select Right Angle Axes.

6. Select **Apply** after changing the settings, and verify the sample.

7. When satisfied, click on **OK**.

MOUSE

Instead of steps 2 to 7, simply click on the chart within the chart window to select it, then drag a corner handle in any direction to change elevation, rotation, and perspective in one step.

TIP

To reset the settings, select **Default**.

Chart—Formatting

Enables you to change the border and fill color of different chart elements. You can also use this command to format all the text elements of a chart by selecting the chart area in step 1. To format text elements separately, see "Chart—Formatting Text." To format a chart automatically, see "Chart— AutoFormat."

EXAMPLE

An Excel chart contains many chart elements, such as the chart area, the plot area (a smaller region whose borders are formed by the axes of the chart), data markers, titles, and legend. You can format any of these items separately, or by selecting the chart area, you can format all the chart items at once.

1. Activate the chart.

2. Double-click on the chart item you want to format.

Instead of steps 2 and 3, select **Format xxxx Area** from the shortcut menu.

3. **(Optional)** Select a border style.

To add a shadow box around the chart, select Shadow.

4. **(Optional)** Select an area color and/or a fill pattern and color.

To create a custom color, select an area color (main color), then select a fill pattern and fill color from the **P**attern palette. For example, to create a deep violet color, select a red area color, then select a dense fill pattern and a blue fill color.

You can change the color of a selected item quickly with the Color and Font Color buttons on the **Formatting** toolbar.

5. **(Optional)** If you selected chart area, you can format all the chart text at once through the **Font** tab.

6. Click on **OK**.

Chart—Formatting Numbers

Formats the numbers in a chart.

1. Double-click on the axis you want to format.

MOUSE

You can also select an axis, and choose **Format Axis** from the shortcut menu.

2. Select the **Number** tab.

3. Choose a number **Category**.

4. Choose a **Format Code**.

5. Click on **OK**.

MOUSE

You can also format numbers in a chart with the number format tools on the **Formatting** toolbar. For example, select an axis and click on the **Currency Style** button.

Chart—Formatting Text

Formats text of individual chart elements, such as the title or the legend. To format all the text in a

*chart in one step, see "Chart—Formatting." To
format numbers in a chart, see "Chart—Formatting
Numbers."*

1. Double-click on the text element you want to
    format.

MOUSE

Instead of step 1, click on the text element
to select it, then choose **Format xxxx**
from the shortcut menu.

2. (**Optional**) Select the **Font** tab and change
    desired text attributes, such as the font or
    point size.

3. (**Optional**) Select the **Alignment** tab and
    change text alignment.

4. (**Optional**) Select the **Patterns** tab and add
    color to text, or a border.

5. Click on **OK**.

MOUSE

You can also change text attributes with
the Formatting toolbar. See *"Cells—
Formatting."*

Chart—Gallery

See "Chart—AutoFormat."

Chart—Gridlines

Displays or hides the Major and Minor gridlines on the active chart. To remove gridlines later on, repeat these steps.

1. Activate the chart.

2. Open the Insert menu.

3. Select Gridlines.

Instead of steps 2 and 3, select **Insert Gridlines** from the shortcut menu.

MOUSE

4. In the **Category (X) axis** box, select Major Gridlines, Minor Gridlines, or both.

5. In the **Value (Y) axis** box, select Major Gridlines, Minor Gridlines, or both.

6. Click on **OK**.

To add horizontal gridlines quickly to a chart, click on the **Horizontal Gridlines** tool on the **Chart** toolbar.

MOUSE

Chart—Legend

*Adds a legend to the active chart. To remove it later on, select it and press **Delete**.*

TIP

A *legend* is simply a box where the data series in the chart are identified.

1. Activate the chart.

2. Open the Insert menu.

3. Select **Legend**.

4. **(Optional)** To reposition the legend, click on the legend and drag it to the desired position.

MOUSE

Click on the **Legend** tool in the **Chart** toolbar to add a legend quickly to the active chart.

Chart—Lines and Bars

Adds additional lines and bars to a chart to empha-size changes in data, such as high/low points. To add error bars (which display the potential error in chart data) or trendlines, see "Chart—Error Bars" or "Chart—Trendlines." To add horizontal lines behind chart data, see "Chart—Gridlines."

1. Activate chart by double-clicking on it, or opening the chart sheet.

2. Open the Format menu.

3. Select the data group you want to change.

EXAMPLE

For example, select **Column** or **Line Group** at the bottom of the menu.

4. Select the **Options** tab.

5. Choose an option (depending on the group type, some options are not available):

   Drop Lines—Vertical lines dropped from data points to the horizontal axis.

   High-Low Lines—Lines connecting the high and low points of data.

   Series Lines—Horizontal lines connecting the high and low points of each series in a stacked bar or column chart.

   Up-Down Bars—Columns showing the relative height of data points on a line chart.

6. Select **OK**.

Chart—Moving

Moves the selected chart to a new location within the worksheet.

1. Click on the chart to select it. Black selection handles will appear around the chart.

2. Drag the chart to the desired location.

Chart—Resizing

See "Chart—Sizing."

Chart—Moving a Chart Object

Allows you to move the objects on a chart.

1. Activate the chart.

2. Click on the chart object you want to move.

3. Drag the object to its new location.

Chart—Printing

Prints the selected chart. If the chart is embedded, you can print it with the worksheet. See "Printing—Worksheet" or "Printing—Workbook." To print just the embedded chart, see "Printing—Setting Print Area." If the chart is contained in its own sheet (chart sheet), it can be resized before printing. Follow these instructions:

1. Move to the chart sheet.

2. Open the File menu.

3. Select Page Setup.

4. On the **Chart** tab, select a sizing option:

   Use Full Page—Changes the proportions of the chart to fit the page.

   Scale to Fit Page—Maintains the chart proportions while scaling it to fit the page.

Custom—Prints the chart, based on its on-screen proportions.

TIP

If you choose Scale to **F**it Page or **C**ustom, a selection border is placed around the chart. You can use this selection border to customize the size and proportions of the chart before printing.

5. Complete any other printing adjustments.

TIP

To print a color chart, deselect Print in **B**lack and White.

6. **(Optional)** Preview the chart before printing by clicking on Print Previe**w**.

7. Print the chart by clicking on **P**rint.

Chart—Protecting

Protects a chart sheet from changes being made to either the data or the formatting, and allows you to add a password. Note: you cannot protect an embedded chart, just the worksheet itself. See "Worksheet—Protecting."

Chart—Scaling

Enables the changing of the scale settings for each chart axis.

Changing the scaling of a chart makes a big difference in impact. By reducing or enlarging the values of the axis, you can make the chart clearer and more concise, bringing dramatic emphasis to the data.

EXAMPLE

1. Activate the chart.

2. Select an axis to scale.

3. Open the Format menu.

4. Choose Selected Axis.

Instead of steps 3 and 4, select **Format Axis** from the shortcut menu.

MOUSE

5. Select the **Scale** tab.

6. Change the desired scaling options.

For example, to limit the size of the scale used, change the minimum and maximum values.

EXAMPLE

7. Click on **OK**.

Chart—Selecting

To select a chart to move its position or change its size, simply click on it. To select a chart so you can edit or format it, see "Chart—Activating."

Here is a list of the objects/areas you can select within a chart:

Chart itself   If the chart is embedded, you can select the chart itself, and then resize or move the chart. Click on the outer border of the chart to select it.

Chart area   The window in which the chart is displayed. By selecting the chart area, you can perform global formatting changes. To select the chart area, click just within the window border, outside of the *plot area*.

Plot area   This is the area bounded by the chart axes. Click within the plot area to select it.

Data markers   Graphic objects that depict the data being charted—for example, the columns of a column chart. To select a data marker, click on it.

Legend   Box which identifies the different series in a chart. To select the legend, click on it.

Title   The title for the chart. To select the chart title, click on it.

Chart—Sizing

Allows the sizing of objects (arrows and unattached text) on the active chart. To change the size of the chart itself, select the entire chart. See "Chart—Selecting."

1. Activate the chart.

2. Select the object you want to size by clicking on it, or select the entire chart. Black handles called *selection handles* will appear along the border of the selected object.

EXAMPLE

For example, click on the plot area.

3. Move the mouse pointer to one of the selection handles. The pointer will change to a two-headed arrow.

4. Drag the borders of the object to resize it. To resize an object proportionally, drag it by a corner handle.

Chart—Spell Checking

Verifies the spelling of any text within a chart. See "Spelling—Checking."

Chart—Text

Adds text to a chart which you specify. To add text to a chart, use a text box. See "Graphic Objects—Creating." To add a title, see "Chart—Titles."

Chart—Titles

Adds a title to the chart itself, the horizontal axis (category), or the vertical axis (values).

1. Activate the chart.

2. Open the Insert menu.

3. Select Titles.

4. Choose a chart element to which to add a title.

5. Click on **OK**.

6. Enter the text for the title ....*title*

Chart—Trendlines

Adds a trendline to a series.

EXAMPLE

A *trendline* can be used to extend data into the future using various prediction methods. A trendline can also be added to existing data to create a *moving average* which smooths out changes in data over time.

TIP

You can't add a trendline to a 3-D, dough-nut, or pie chart.

1. Activate the chart.

2. Select the series to which you want to add a trendline.

3. Open the Insert menu.

4. Select Trendline.

5. Under the **Type** tab, select a Trend/Regression Type.

6. (**Optional**) If you selected **P**olynominal, choose the highest power for the variables used in the prediction calculation.

7. (**Optional**) If you selected **M**oving Average, indicate the number of months to be used.

8. (**Optional**) To forecast into the future (or back to the past), select the **Options** tab and indicate the number of periods to be used.

9. (**Optional**) To name your trendline, select the **Options** tab and enter a name.

10. Click on **OK**.

Chart—Unprotecting

Does not protect the active protected chart which has been given a password. Note: you cannot protect an embedded chart, just the worksheet itself, so a protected chart is one stored in its own protected worksheet. To protect such a chart, see "Worksheet—Protecting."

Column—Changing Width

Changes the width of a column to accommodate more data. To hide columns by changing their width, see "View—Hiding Cells."

TIP

If a column is too small to display all the contents of a cell, you will see pound signs (####) in the cell. The data remains intact, and is displayed in full if you widen the column.

1. Select a cell from each column (or a range of columns) whose width you want to change. To select a column, click on the column heading. To select multiple columns, simply drag over the headings. To select non-contiguous columns, press **Ctrl** as you click on each heading.

MOUSE

You can change column width for an entire worksheet by clicking on the **Select All** button.

2. Move the mouse pointer to the right border of a column. The pointer will change to two vertical lines.

3. Drag the border to adjust its size. If multiple columns are selected, this will adjust all the columns at once.

MOUSE

If you want to adjust the column to the size of its data ("best fit"), double-click on the right border.

TIP

To reset a column to standard width, select it, then open the Format menu. Select Column, then choose Standard Width. Click on **OK** to accept the standard measurement.

Column—Deleting

See "Cells—Deleting."

Column—Inserting

See "Cells—Inserting."

Column—Hiding

See "View—Hiding Cells."

Column—Selecting

See "Selecting—Columns."

Data—Aligning in a Cell

See "Cells—Aligning Data."

Data—Changing the Appearance of

See "Cells—Changing the Appearance of Text" or "Cells—Changing the Appearance of Numbers."

Data—Clearing

See "Cells—Clearing."

Data—Copying

Copies data in selected cell(s) to the Windows Clipboard. The copied selections can consist of data, text, formulas, a chart, or a graphic object; they can occupy a single cell, a range, or the entire document. Once the data is copied to the Clipboard, use the Paste command to copy the data to the current Excel worksheet, another worksheet, or another application's document. To copy only the format (and not the data in the cell), see "Cells—Copying the Format of." To copy data from another application, or to insert copied cells between cells on the worksheet, see "Data—Pasting" and "Data—Inserting Copied or Cut Cells."

TIP

The look of your data can differ slightly, depending on the application you paste it into. Microsoft Word, for example, puts the data in a table.

When you copy cells containing formulas, be careful about how cells are referenced in the formulas. If a formula contains **absolute references**, *any copy of your formula will be identical to the original, no matter where you copy it to.* **Relative references** *mean the references in a copy of the formula will change, depending on where you place the copy. For example, if you have a formula that has a relative reference to cell A1, and you copy the formula to a cell one row down and one column to the right, the relative reference will change to cell B2. For more information, see "Formula—Absolute and Relative References."*

Mouse Steps

1. Select the cell(s) to copy.

2. Click on the **fill handle**.

3. Drag down or to the right.

To copy cells, click on the **Copy** button on the **Standard** toolbar. To paste, click on the **Paste** button. You can also select the Copy and **Paste** commands from the shortcut menu.

You can also copy by dragging. Select the cells you want to copy. Point to the selection border; press and hold the **Ctrl** key until a small plus (+) pointer appears. Drag to a new location, and then release the mouse button and **Ctrl** key.

Keyboard Steps

1. Select the cell(s) to copy into
   the Clipboard .... **Shift** + **↑** **↓** **←** **→**

2. Open the Edit menu .... **Alt** + **E**

3. Select Copy .... **C**

TIP

You can also press **Ctrl+C** to copy the
selection to the Clipboard.

4. Select a new location to which
   the selected cell(s) will
   be copied .... **↑** **↓** **←** **→**

5. Open the Edit menu .... **Alt** + **E**

6. Select **Paste** .... **P**

TIP

You can paste the contents of the Clipboard quickly by pressing **Enter** in place
of steps 5–7.

7. To stop the flashing marquee, press .... **Esc**

Data—Copying the Format of

See "Cells—Copying the Format of."

Data—Cutting and Pasting

Removes the selected cell or range of cells from the worksheet, and places them in the Windows Clipboard. You can then use the Paste or Paste Special command to place the data somewhere else on the same worksheet, on a different worksheet, in a different workbook, or in another application.

If you are moving cells that contain formulas, be careful with the cell references. Although Excel may adjust the cell references for you, those adjustments may not be the ones you want. For more information, see "Formula—Absolute and Relative References."

EXAMPLE You may decide to move a range of cells down on a worksheet to make room for a heading or title you forget to add. If you used formulas in the range you want to move, Excel will adjust any cell references in the formulas to insert the correct results. In such a case, you would have problems only if you used an absolute cell reference (one that has dollar signs, such as $A12 or $B$13).

1. Select the cell(s) to cut.

2. Open the Edit menu .... Alt + E

3. Select Cut .... T

4. Choose destination cell (or range) as the new location for the selected cell(s) .... ↑ ↓ ← →

5. Open the Edit menu ....

6. Select **Paste** .... P

TIP A quick way to cut a selection to the Clipboard is to press **Ctrl+X** or click on the **Cut** button in the **Standard** toolbar (the button with the scissors on it). To paste the cut data, select the cell or range where you want the Clipboard contents pasted, and press **Ctrl+V** or click on the **Paste** button (the button with the clipboard on it).

TIP To bypass the Edit menu, use the shortcut menu. Select the cells to Cut, then right-click on one of the selected cells, and choose Cut. Right-click on the cell where you want the cut data pasted, and choose **Paste**.

MOUSE You can also cut and paste cells using Drag and Drop. Select the cells you want to move. Move the tip of the mouse pointer over the selected cells' border, so the mouse pointer turns into an arrow. Hold down the left mouse button, drag the selection to a new location, and release the mouse button.

Data—Deleting

See "Cells—Clearing."

Data—Editing in a Cell

Allows you to change the entry inside a cell.

Mouse Steps

1. Click inside the cell you want to edit.

2. Click inside the entry on the **formula bar**.

3. Type your changes.

4. Click on the **Enter** button (the button with the checkmark on it).

Keyboard Steps

1. Select the cell you want to edit ...↑ ↓ ← →

2. Press **F2** F2

3. Use the **arrow** keys to move
   the insertion point.................................← →

4. Type your changes ....Back Delete
   text

5. Press **Enter** ....↵

TIP

Double-click inside the cell whose entry you want to edit. This places the insertion point inside the cell, allowing you to edit the entry.

TIP

To replace an entry in a cell, select the cell and type the new entry. The new entry replaces the old one.

Data—Entering Labels, Values, and Dates

Lets you type text, numbers, and dates into a cell. For information on entering formulas into cells, see "Formula—Creating." For information on entering functions, see "Functions—Inserting with Function Wizard."

1. Click on the desired cell.

2. Type your entry:

   Type the text entry. To treat a number (such as an address or ZIP code) as text, type an apostrophe (') first. .... Text

   Type the number, including any decimal points to be added. To add symbols, such as $ or %, you can apply a number format later. See *Cells—Changing the Appearance of Numbers.*" .... Number

   Type the date in one of these formats: ..... Date

   MM/DD/YY
   MMM–YY
   DD–MMM–YY
   DD–MMM

3. Click on the **Enter** button (the button with the checkmark on it), or press **Enter**.

TIP

To type the same entry in several cells, select the cells, type your entry, and press **Ctrl+Enter**.

Data—Finding

Searches an entire workbook or a selected range for specified text or values.

1. Select the cells you want to search:

   Select any cell in the worksheet, but select only one cell. ....Entire worksheet

   Select only those cells you want to search. See *"Selecting—Cells and Ranges."* ....Selected range

   Select every worksheet you want to search. See *"Selecting—Worksheets."* ....Several worksheets

2. Open the **Edit** menu and choose **Find** ....**Alt**+**E** **F**

3. In the **Find** What box, enter the data to search for ....**Alt**+**N**
   text or *number*

EXAMPLE You can use wildcard characters to stand in for other characters. Use * for a group of characters or ? for single characters. For example, to find Book or Cook, type **?oo?**. To find all entries that start with K, type **K***.

4. Select Match **C**ase to search for entries that exactly match the capitalization used in the Find What box .... `Alt`+`C`

5. Select Find Entire Cells **O**nly to have Excel look for exact, complete matches for the entry you typed .... `Alt`+`O`

6. From the **S**earch list, choose **By Rows** or **By Columns** .... `Alt`+`S`

7. From the **L**ook in list, choose **Formulas**, **Values**, or **Notes** .... `Alt`+`L`

8. Click on the **F**ind Next button .... `Alt`+`F`

9. To move to the next occurrence of the item, click on **F**ind Next .... `Alt`+`F`

10. Click on **Close** .... `Esc`

Data—Inserting Copied or Cut Cells

Inserts the Clipboard contents (cells, ranges, rows, or columns) between existing cells. Existing cells will shift to accommodate the insertion.

1. Use the **E**dit **C**opy or the **E**dit **Cu**t command to place selected cells into the Clipboard.

2. Select the cell in the upper left corner of the range into which you want the copied or cut cells pasted.

3. Open the **I**nsert menu .... `Alt`+`I`

4. Select Copied or Cut C**e**lls .... `E`

5. Select one of the following options:
   Shift Cells **R**ight .... `Alt`+`R`

   Shift Cells **D**own .... `Alt`+`D`

6. Select **OK** .... `⏎`

Data—Moving

See "Data—Cutting and Pasting."

Data—Pasting

Copies (pastes) the contents of the Windows Clipboard into a specified cell or range of cells, replacing any data that may already exist in the target cells.

TIP

The Windows Clipboard is used as temporary storage for all your Windows applications, **so** you can use it to transfer data from another application to Excel. Simply select and copy the data in the other program, and then paste it into your Excel workbook. To learn how to link the data from the other program to the pasted data, refer to *"Data—Paste Special."*

If you are moving cells that contain formulas, be careful with the cell references. Although Excel may adjust the cell references for you, those adjustments may not be the ones you want. After pasting the formulas, check them to make sure the cell references have been adjusted correctly. For more information, see "Formula—Creating" and "Formula—Absolute and Relative References."

1. Use the **Edit Copy** or **Edit Cut** command to place selected cells into the Clipboard.

2. Select the cell in the upper left corner of the range into which you want to paste the copied or cut cells.

TIP

You can also open another Excel worksheet or workbook (or go to another application), and paste the contents of the Clipboard there.

3. Open the **Edit** menu and select **Paste**, or (to bypass the menu) press ....

TIP

To bypass the **Edit** menu, use the shortcut menu. Select the cells you want to copy or move, and then right-click on one of the selected cells, and choose **C**opy or Cu**t**. Right-click where you want the cells copied or moved, and choose **P**aste.

MOUSE

A quick way to copy or move selected cells with a mouse is to use the Drag and Drop feature. To move cells, select the cells, drag the selection border to where you want the cells moved, and release the mouse button. To copy cells, hold down the **Ctrl** key while dragging.

Data—Paste Special

Lets you paste only the formulas, formats, values, or notes from the copied cells; gives you greater control over the paste operation.

1. Use the **Edit C**opy command to place the contents and formatting of the selected cells into the Clipboard.

2. Select the cell in the upper left corner of the range into which you want the copied or cut cells pasted.

3. Open the Edit menu .... `Alt`+`E`

4. Select Paste Special .... `S`

5. In the Paste group, select the item you want to paste into the target cell(s).

EXAMPLE If you want to copy several numbers from one workbook to another, but you do not want to copy the formatting that is applied to those numbers, select Values.

6. In the **Operation** group, select an operation you want to perform using copied and targeted cells.

EXAMPLE If you selected a target area that contains values, you can select Add in the **Operation** group to have Excel add the values from the copied cells to the values in the target cells, and paste the result into the target cells.

7. Choose Skip Blanks to prevent Excel from pasting blank cells to the target area .... `Alt`+`B`

8. Choose Transpose to have Excel
   paste columns as rows and
   rows as columns ....

9. Select **OK** ....

TIP

To paste an item that you copied in
another application, click on the Paste
Link button to establish a link between
the source data and the copy. Now,
whenever you edit the source data (using
the other application), those changes are
reflected in the pasted data.

Data—Replacing

*Searches an entire document or a selected range for
specified text or values, and replaces the found
data with other text or values you specify.*

1. Select the cells whose entries you want to
   replace:

   Select any cell in the worksheet, but select
   only one cell. ....Entire worksheet

   Select only those cells you want to search.
   See *"Selecting—Cells and Ranges."* .... Selected
   range

   Select every worksheet you want to search.
   See *"Selecting—Worksheets."* .... Several
   worksheets

2. Open the Edit menu and
   choose Replace .... `Alt`+`E`
                                                         `E`

3. In the Find What box, enter
   the data to search for .... `Alt`+`N`
   text* or *number

4. In the Replace with box, type the
   replacement entry .... `Alt`+`E`
   replacement text

5. From the Search list, choose
   By Rows or **By Columns** .... `Alt`+`S`

6. Select Match Case to replace
   entries that match exactly
   the capitalization used
   in the Find What box.......................... `Alt`+`C`

7. Select Find Entire Cells Only
   to have Excel replace exact,
   complete matches for
   the entry you typed .... `Alt`+`O`

8. Select any of the following options:

   To Replace All of the matches,
   press .... `Alt`+`A`

   To skip the current cell and
   find the next occurrence,
   select Find Next................................. `Alt`+`F`

To replace the contents of the
current cell and find the next
occurrence, select **R**eplace .... `Alt`+`R`

9. When finished replacing,
   select **Close** .... `Esc`

Data—Protecting

See "Cells—Protecting."

Data—Styles

See "Styles—Applying" and "Styles—Creating."

Data List—Adding a Record

*Allows you to add a record to an existing data list by
filling in the blanks in a data form. For details on
creating a data list, refer to "Data List—Creating."*

1. Select any cell in the data list.

2. Open the **D**ata menu and
   select **F**orm .... `Alt`+`D`
   `O`

3. Select Ne**w** .... `Alt`+`W`

4. Type an entry into each of the text
   boxes. (Press **Tab** or point and
   click to move from box to box.) ...***text entries***

5. Repeat steps 3 and 4 for each new record you want to add.

6. Select Close .... Alt + L

Data List—Analyzing Data

See "Data List—Subtotals" and "Pivot Table—Creating from a Data List."

Data List—Creating

*Makes a list that you can use to store, retrieve, and analyze data. A **data list** is really a database without the fancy terminology. The topmost row contains the column labels (field names). Each row contains a record made up of several field entries.*

EXAMPLE You can use a data list to store names and addresses of friends and clients, sales figures, budget information, or even checkbook entries.

1. Type a row of column labels.

EXAMPLE The column labels indicate the type of data in each column. For example, to create an address list, you might type column labels such as **Last Name**, **First Name**, **Address**, **City**, **State**, **ZIP Code**, and **Phone Number**.

2. Format the column headings to make them stand out. The character format must differ from the format used in the remaining rows.

3. Type data entries in following rows. Do not leave a blank row between the column label row and the first data row.

4. Repeat step 3 to enter all your data. Keep your list on a single worksheet.

Data List—Data Form

Displays each record in your data list on a separate "page," allowing you to find, edit, add, and delete individual records. To learn how to create a data list, see "Data List—Creating." The following options are available in the Data Form.

Data Form Dialog Box Buttons

Button	Description
Close	Closes the Data Form dialog box.
Criteria	Displays a dialog box you can use to search for specific records.
Delete	Deletes the selected record.
Find Next	Finds the next matching record after criteria are specified.
Find Prev	Finds the previous matching record after criteria are specified.
Form	(Appears when you select Criteria) Returns to the Data Form.
New	Adds a new record.
Restore	Restores data to its state prior to editing.

Button	Description
Clear	Appears when you select **Criteria**; clears the current entry from the Criteria form.

1. Select any cell in your data list.

2. Open the **D**ata menu and
   select **F**orm .... `Alt`+`D`
   `O`

3. When viewing, adding, editing,
   or deleting a database record,
   select one of the buttons in
   the preceding table
   by pressing .... `Alt`+*selection letter*

4. When finished with Data Form,
   select C**l**ose .... `Alt`+`L` or `Esc`

Data List—Deleting a Record

Deletes a single record from a data list.

1. Select any cell in the data list.

2. Open the **D**ata menu and
   select **F**orm .... `Alt`+`D`
   `O`

3. Display the record you want
   to delete.

4. Click on the **D**elete button .... `Alt`+`D`

5. Click on the **OK** button .... `↵`

> **TIP** To delete more than one record at a time, select the records in the list, and use the **Edit** **D**elete command to delete the records.

Data List—Editing a Record

Lets you change a record using the Data Form dialog box.

1. Select any cell in the data list.

2. Open the **D**ata menu and select
   Form .... `Alt`+`D`
   `O`

3. Display the record you want to edit.

4. Edit any field entry:

   Tab to the entry you want to
   replace, and type the new
   entry .... Replace entry

   Tab to the entry you want to edit, use
   the **arrow** keys to move the insertion
   point, and type your change .... Edit entry

   To cancel your changes, click on
   the **R**estore button .... Cancel edit

5. Move to the next record you want
   to edit, or choose Close.

TIP

You can edit field entries as you would
edit the contents of any cell. Select the cell
and press **F2** (or click on the entry in the
formula bar), or double-click on the cell.
Then move the insertion point. Type your
changes.

Data List—Filtering with Advanced Filter

*Lets you filter a list using more than one field and
(optionally) copy the filtered list to a different
worksheet or different location on the same
worksheet. A simpler way to filter a list is to use
AutoFilter; see "Data List—Filtering with
AutoFilter."*

The first step consists of typing (on a separate
area of the worksheet called the criteria range) the
column headings and criteria you want to use to
narrow the list. (The criteria range must have at least
one blank row or column between it and the data
list.) You can enter criteria for one or more fields.

EXAMPLE

To search for all people whose last names
begin with K-Z *and* who live in Chicago,
enter the criteria in the same row:

Last Name City
>=K   Chicago

To search for all people whose last names begin
with K-Z *or* who live in Chicago, enter the criteria on
separate rows:

Last Name   **City**
$>=K$

                      Chicago

1. On a separate section of the work-
    sheet, type the desired criteria.

TIP

You can copy and paste column headings
from your data list to a separate area of
your worksheet to create a criteria range.
Be sure you leave an empty row or
column between your criteria range and
your data list.

2. Select any cell in the data list, not in
    the criteria range.

3. Open the **D**ata menu and select
    Filter .... Alt + D
                                                          F

4. Select A**d**vanced Filter .... A

5. In the Action group, choose .... Alt + F
                                   or Alt + O

    To hide any records in the list that do not match
    your criteria. This does not create a
    separate, filtered list .... Filter the List, in-place

To create a separate, filtered list and place it on another worksheet or in a different location on this worksheet .... Copy to Another Location

6. Make sure the range in the **List Range** text box matches the range of your data list ....

7. In the **Criteria Range** text box, type the range of cells that contain the criteria you typed in step 1 .... **Alt** + **C**

> **TIP**
> You can type a range or drag over the range with a mouse. As you drag, the dialog box remains on-screen.

8. If you chose to copy the filtered list to another location, in step 5, choose Copy **to**, and type a range where you want the filtered list placed ....

> **TIP**
> You can type a range or the address of a single cell. Excel will copy the filtered list to that cell, and any additional cells down and to the right of the cell you specify. You can also select a cell or range with your mouse.

9. Click on **OK** ....

Data List—Filtering with AutoFilter

Displays only the portion of the data list you specify. For more advanced filtering options, see "Data List—Filtering with Advanced Filter."

1. Select any cell in the list.

2. From the Data menu select Filter .... [Alt]+[D]
                                                    [F]

3. Select AutoFilter ....[F]

4. Click on the drop-down list button for the column you want to use to filter the list.

5. Select the entry you want to use to narrow your list.

EXAMPLE To display the records for all people who live in Boston, you would pull down the **City** drop-down list and select **Boston**.

6. (**Optional**) You can repeat steps 4 and 5 to further narrow the list.

TIP To unfilter a list, select (**All**) at the top of the filtered column's drop-down list. To turn AutoFilter off, select **Data Filter** AutoFilter.

Sometimes you may not want to filter a list by using exact matches. For example, you may want to view records for people whose last name starts with K through R. In such a case, you can create a *custom filter*.

1. Click on the drop-down list button for the column you want to use to filter the list.

2. Select **(Custom...)**.

3. Enter your AutoFilter criteria. You can type entries or select them from the drop-down lists.

EXAMPLE
For example, to view all records for those people whose last name starts with K through R, you would enter **>K**, select **And**, and enter **<S**.

4. Click on the **OK** button ....

Data List—Finding a Record

Locates an individual record in a data list, and displays the data in the Data Form dialog box. For information on how to create a data list, see "Data List—Creating." To use the Find feature to search for an individual cell entry, see "Data—Finding."

EXAMPLE

Search criteria tells Excel which field to look in, and which entry to look for in that field. For example, to find all records that have a last-name entry starting with K, you would type **K** in the **Last Name** field. To find records whose last name entry starts with a letter after K, you would type **>K** (greater than K) in the **Last Name** field.

You can use wildcard characters and relative operators to broaden your search, as listed in this table:

Entry   What It Does

Wildcard Character

*   Stands in for any group of characters.

?   Stands in for a single character.

Relative Operators

\>   Greater Than—Finds all records that have entries greater than the one you type.

<   Less Than—Finds all records that have entries less than the one you type.

\>=   Greater Than or Equal To—Finds all records that have entries that match or are greater than the one you type.

<=   Less Than or Equal To—Finds all records that have entries that match or are less than the one you type.

<>   Not Equal To—Finds all records that do not match the entry you type.

1. Select any cell in the data list.

2. From the **D**ata menu select **F**orm .... [Alt] + [D]
   [O]

3. Select **C**riteria .... [Alt] + [C]

4. Type a search entry into one or
   more of the text boxes .... ***text entries***

5. Select Find **N**ext .... [Alt] + [N]

6. Select Find **N**ext to find the next
   record that matches your entry .... [Alt] + [N]

You can also find a record by flipping through
the records using the Data Form dialog box. With the
dialog box on-screen, press [↑] or [↓] to view the
previous or next record, or use the **scroll bar** to flip
from one record to the next.

Data List—Sorting a List

*Organizes the list as specified from A to Z, Z to A,
1 to 10, or 10 to 1. To sort a list, you enter two
instructions. You tell Excel which field to sort by
(for example, Last Name) and which sort order to
use: Ascending (A to Z or 1 to 10) or Descending (Z
to A or 10 to 1). You can sort using up to three fields
(sort keys).*

EXAMPLE

If you wanted a list of your clients alpha-
betized by city, and then by last name and
first name, you would use a ***three-key
sort***. The *1st key* is the key that all records
are sorted on, the City field. All records
that have the same city are sorted by the

2nd key, the last-name field. Finally, if there are records that have the same city and the same last name, these records are sorted by the *3rd key*, the first-name field.

1. Select any cell in your data list.

2. Open the **Data** menu and select
    Sort ....**Alt**+**D**
    S

3. Open the **S**ort By drop-down list,
    and select the first column you
    want to sort on ....**Alt**+**S**

To sort by last name, select the **Last Name** column from the Sort By drop-down list.

EXAMPLE

4. Click on **A**scending or **D**escending to specify a sort order.

5. To sort on another field, repeat steps 3 and 4 for the first and second **Then By** drop-down lists.

6. Click on **OK** ....**↵**

You can undo a sort by opening the **Edit** menu and selecting Undo Sort or by clicking on the **Undo** button in the **Standard** toolbar.

TIP

TIP

To sort a list by a single column (say Last Names), select a cell in that column, and then click on the **Sort Ascending** or **Sort Descending** button in the **Standard** toolbar.

Data List—Subtotals

Calculates totals, grand totals, and averages in a list automatically, without requiring you to enter a single formula or function. Subtotals provide a simple way to summarize and analyze data. For more complex data analysis, use a pivot table; for more information, see "Pivot Table—Creating from a Data List."

EXAMPLE

The only difficulty with subtotals is deciding what you want to subtotal. If you have total-sales figures, for example, you can sort the list by quarter, by salesperson, or by region. For details on how to sort a list, refer to *"Data List—Sorting a List."*

1. Sort the list.

2. Select any cell in the list.

3. Open the **D**ata menu and select Su**b**totals .... Alt + D
                                                                                        B

4. Open the **A**t Each Change in list, and choose the field whose items you want to subtotal.

EXAMPLE

For example, to determine a subtotal for salespeople, select the **Salesperson** field.

5. Open the Use Function list, and choose the mathematical operation you want to perform.

EXAMPLE

For example, you can choose **Sum** to determine totals, **Average** to determine averages, or **Count** to determine how many items you have in the list.

6. In the Add Subtotal to group, choose every column for which you want a subtotal.

7. Select any other options as desired.

8. Click on the **OK** button ....

TIP

If you added a title at the top of your list (in addition to the column label rows), you may get a dialog box saying that there is a header at the top of the list and asking if you want to extend the selection over the header. Answer **No**. (If you answer Yes, Excel assumes that the title is a column label, and the subtotals will not work correctly.)

When Excel creates a subtotaled table, it displays outline symbols to the left of the table. You can use these symbols to hide or display detail:

The number buttons (at the top of the outline area) control the detail for the entire list. Click on **1** to see the least detail or **3** to see the most detail .... [1][2][3]

Click on a **minus button** to see less detail .... [-]

Plus signs appear when you click on a minus button to see less detail. To see more detail, click on a **plus button** .... [+]

Database

See "Data List" and "Microsoft Query."

Database—Extracting Data

There are several ways to extract data from a data list or database. Choose the procedure that does what you need to do:

Use AutoFilter, as explained in *"Data List—Filtering with Auto-Filter."* .... Narrow a List

Use the Advanced Filter feature, as explained in *"Data List—Filtering with Advanced Filter."* .... Narrow a List and Extract Data

Use Microsoft Query, as explained in
*"MSQuery—Querying a
Database Using Microsoft
Query."* .. Get data from two or more workbooks

If you need to get data from a database created
with Paradox, dBASE, or FoxPro, you can use
Microsoft Query, as explained in *"MSQuery —
Querying a database using Microsoft
Query."* ....Get data from an outside source

Display Options—Changing

See "View—Changing the Display Options."

Drawing Tools

See *"Graphic Objects—Creating."*

Editing Cell Entries

See "Data—Editing in a Cell."

Editing Database Records

See "Data List—Editing a Record."

Embedded Objects—Creating

*Inserts data from another application that supports
OLE (object linking and embedding). For informa-
tion on linking objects, see "Links—Creating" and
"Links—Updating."*

TIP

An *embedded object* becomes part of the workbook in which you place it. A *linked object* remains in its own file, but whenever the workbook is opened, Excel retrieves the object and inserts it temporarily into the workbook as you specified. That way, when you change the source file, the data is updated automatically in the workbook.

To embed an object, cut it from another Windows application and paste it into an Excel workbook. Or do the same thing using the **Insert Object** command. The kind of object you can insert depends on the applications loaded on your system.

1. Open the Insert menu .... **Alt** + **I**

2. Select **Object** .... **O**

3. Click on one of the following tabs, and take the actions:

   Create New Runs an application *so you can* create an object to insert. Select the application you want to run, and choose .... **OK**

   Create from File Inserts an existing file as an embedded object. Select a file to insert, and select .... **OK**

4. If you ran an application, use the application to create the object.

TIP

Depending on the object you are inserting, more steps may be needed to create the object. For example, to insert a drawn object, you'll need to draw it first.

5. After creating the object,
   open the program's File menu .... `Alt`+`F`

> **TIP**
> With some applications and *applets*
> (small applications that create insertable
> objects), you won't have a File menu.
> You simply create the object, and then
> click anywhere outside it to exit the
> application.

6. Select Exit & Return to ....`X`

7. Select Yes ....`←`

Embedded Objects—Editing

*Edits an object embedded in an Excel workbook. To
copy, move, resize, shape, or delete an embedded
object, see "Graphic Objects."*

1. Double-click on the object.

2. Edit the object in the application
   used to create it.

3. Select Exit & Return to ....`X`

4. Select Yes ....`←`

Exiting

*Closes all open workbooks, exits Excel, and returns
you to the Windows Program Manager.*

1. Open the File menu ....`Alt`+`F`

2. Select Exit ....`X`

TIP

If you exit from an open workbook and have not saved it, Excel will ask whether you want to save it. Select **Yes** to save, or **No** to not save.

TIP

To bypass the **File** menu, press **Alt+F4** or double-click on the **Control-menu box** in the upper left corner of the Microsoft Excel window.

File—Closing

See "Window—Closing."

File—Finding

Locates misplaced files. The File Find feature searches for files by name and content. File Find will search for exact matches, or you can use wildcard characters (* and ?) to broaden the search.

EXAMPLE

Use an asterisk (*) in place of a group of characters, or use a question mark (?) in place of a single character. For example, ***.xls** finds all files with the extension .xls, and **sales??.xls** finds all files, such as SALES01.XLS, SALES02.XLS, and so on.

1. Open the File menu .... **Alt**+**F**

2. Select Find File .... **F**

EXAMPLE If you select **F**ind File, and you get the Find File dialog box instead of the Search dialog box, click on the **S**earch button to display the Search dialog box.

3. Go to the File **N**ame text box .... Alt + N

4. Type the name of the file you want to find .... *filename*

5. Go to the **L**ocation text box .... Alt + L

6. Type the drive and directory to search .... *text entry*

7. (Optional)Select the Include Su**b**directories check box to have Excel search all subdirectories of the drive you specify .... Alt + B

8. Select the **R**ebuild File List check box .... Alt + R

9. Click on **OK** .... ⏎

TIP If you get unexpected results, perform the search again, and make sure there is an X in the **R**ebuild File List check box. Other-wise, Excel searches only the list of found files in the Find File dialog box.

TIP Some dialog boxcs, including the Open dialog box, contain a **F**ind File button. You can click on this button to search for a file, rather than selecting **F**ile **F**ind File.

File—New

See "Workbook—New."

File—Opening

See "Workbook—Opening."

File—Saving

See "Workbook—Saving."

File—Saving a Copy of

See "Workbook—Saving with a New Name."

Find and Replace

See "Data—Finding" and "Data—Replacing."

Format Painter

See "Cells—Copying the Format of."

Formatting—Cells and Data

Refer to "Cells—Adding Borders," "Cells—Aligning Data," "Cells—Changing the Appearance of Text," "Cells—Changing the Appearance of Numbers," "Cells—Protecting," "AutoFormat," "Column—Changing Width," and "Row—Changing Height."

Formula—Absolute and Relative References

*When you put cell addresses in a formula, Excel inserts the addresses automatically as **relative references** (the cell references change if you move or copy the cell). For information on how to enter a formula, see "Formula—Creating." To use cell names rather than addresses, see "Names—Defining Cell and Range Names" and "Formula—Using Named Cells and Ranges."*

EXAMPLE

You've created the formula =(A1+A2) in cell A3. Now you want to add the numbers in cells B1 and B2. When you copy cell A3 to B3, Excel adjusts the formula to add B1 and B2 instead of A1 and A2. In cell B3, you'll see the formula =(B1+B2).

If you want cell references in a formula to stay the same when you copy or move the formula, make the references *absolute*. If the references are relative, they will change to become relative to the new position when copied or moved.

EXAMPLE

If a cell holds the formula =SUM(A1:A9) (for the sum of all your column A numbers), and you copy it to a cell in column B, Excel adjusts the formula to add all the numbers in column B; now it reads =SUM(B1:B9). If you want Excel to keep the original cell references, no matter where you copy the formula, make them absolute; insert dollar signs before the column letters and row numbers: =SUM($A$1:$A$9).

1. Select the cell in which to
    enter a formula.

2. Press the = (equals sign) ....

3. Enter the formula. To make a
    cell address absolute, put a $
    (dollar sign) before its column
    letter and/or row number ....*formula*

TIP

To have Excel convert a relative cell
reference to absolute, first enter the cell's
address, and then press **F4**—once to
make both the column letter and row
number absolute, twice for only the row
number, three times for only the column
letter, and four times to cancel.

4. Click on the **Enter** button (the button
    with the check mark on it)or press **Enter** .... ⏎

Formula—Adding Numbers

See "AutoSum" and "Data List—Subtotals."

Formula—Creating

*Worksheets use formulas to perform calculations on
the data you enter. Formulas must begin with an =
(equal sign); typically they contain one or more cell
addresses and/or values, plus a mathematical operator. You can also use Excel's predefined formulas
(functions) instead of creating your own. See "Functions—Inserting with the Function Wizard."*

Operator	Description
+	Addition
-	Subtraction
*	Multiplication
/	Division
%	Percent
^	Exponent

Excel performs calculations from left to right, doing exponents first, multiplication and division second, and addition and subtraction last. You may have to group parts of the calculation in parentheses to have Excel determine the correct result.

EXAMPLE

You want to know what your home's average monthly utility bills were last year. Cell B1 contains the total electric bill ($500) and cell B2 contains the total gas bill ($350). You want the average to be placed in cell B3. The formula in cell B3 to calculate this average would look like **=(B1+B2)/12**, with the result of **$70.83**. Notice the parentheses ( ). If you did not include the parentheses, B2 would first be divided by 12 and then added to B1 which would result in the total of $529.17.

1. Select the cell where you want the result of the formula to appear.

2. Type an = (equals sign) .... =

3. Type a cell address for the first number in the formula ....*cell address*

MOUSE

Instead of typing cell addresses, you can click on (or drag over) cells to insert their cell addresses into the formula.

4. Enter a mathematical operator (see table on page 91.)

5. Repeat steps 3 and 4 to complete your formula.

6. When finished with the formula, press **Enter** ....

TIP

To enter a cell range, type a colon (:) between the first and last cells in the range. For example, to calculate the sum of values in cells B1 through B12, enter the formula **=SUM(B1:B12)**. To have Excel insert the colon for you, drag the mouse over the range.

For information on how Excel handles cell references when formulas are moved or copied to a different location, see *"Formula—Absolute and Relative References."*

Formula—Entering 3-D References

Allows your formulas to use cell references that refer to cells on different worksheets. To refer to cells in other workbooks, see "Formula—Entering Linking References."

EXAMPLE

You manage three retail stores, and you keep each store's monthly sales figures on a different worksheet: Sheet1, Sheet2, and Sheet3. On Sheet4, you want to keep track of the total sales figures for three stores. You can use 3-D references to do that. Sheet4 might contain a formula that adds the values from cell A15 on worksheets 1, 2, and 3, such as: **Sheet1!A15+Sheet2!A15+Sheet3!A15**.

1. Select the cell in which to enter a formula.

2. Type an = (equals sign) .... =

3. Enter the formula. (For each cell address on a different worksheet, type the worksheet number or name, then an exclamation point, then the cell address) ....*formula*

MOUSE

To have Excel insert the worksheet number and cell address for you, click on the worksheet's tab and then select the cell. Make sure you type mathematical operators between cell references as needed.

4. Click on the **Enter** button (the button with the check mark on it) or press **Enter**. ....

Formula—Entering Linking References

Adds cell references that refer to cells in other workbooks.

EXAMPLE You manage a production company, and you keep your inventory data and production data in separate workbooks. You want to pull information from the inventory workbook (such as cost of parts) and from the production workbook (such as cost per hour) to determine how much it would cost you to make a product. You need a formula that refers to cells in both workbooks.

1. Open the workbooks you want to link.

TIP When moving back and forth between workbooks, it helps to arrange the workbook windows so you can see all of them. Open the **Window** menu, choose **Arrange**, select the desired layout, and click on **OK**.

2. Start creating your formula.

3. To refer to a cell or range in another workbook, click on the cell or drag over the range.

4. To return to the window in which you are creating the formula, click on its title bar.

5. Repeat steps 3 and 4 for each

cell reference you include. (Remember: type a
mathematical operator between references.)

6. When the formula is complete,
    select the **Enter** button
    (the button with the
    check mark on it), or press ....

If you enter changes to the source workbooks, a
dialog box will appear when you open the workbook that contains the linking formula. It asks
whether you want to update the links. Select **Yes**.
For more information about updating links, see
"Links—Updating."

TIP

Instead of selecting cells in other workbooks, you can type the linking reference
yourself. Type the location and name of
the workbook file before the Sheet
number. For example,

'C:\SALES\[SALES02.XLS]Sheet1'!A12

Note that the workbook name is enclosed
in square brackets [] and that an apostro-
phe is inserted before the disk letter and
after the worksheet number. Capitaliza-
tion does not matter.

Formula—Functions

*See "Functions—Inserting with the Function
Wizard."*

Formula—Goal Seeking

A formula usually performs mathematical operations using known values to determine a result. Sometimes, however, you know the result (a goal value), and you want to determine the value needed to arrive at it. The Goal Seeking feature does this for you, so you don't have to use trial and error.

EXAMPLE

You want to purchase a house in the next 5 years, and you want to have $15,000 for the down payment. With the Goal Seeking feature, you could enter a formula in cell C4 that reads **=A4*12*5**. This takes the unknown value in A4 (the monthly amount) and multiplies it by 12 payments per year for 5 years. You use the Goal Seeking feature to determine the amount you need in A4 to come up with a result of 15000.

1. Enter the formula you want to use for goal seeking; it will refer to a cell that does not yet contain a value.

2. Select the cell that contains the formula.

3. Open the Tools menu .... Alt + T

4. Select Goal Seek .... G

5. Go to the To value box .... Alt + V

6. Enter the goal .... *value*

7. Go to the By changing cell box........... Alt + C

8. Enter the cell address of the value
   you want to change (that of the
   unknown value) ....***cell address***

9. Select **OK**... ↵

10. To accept the change select **OK** .... ↵

    OR

    To reject the change,
    select **Cancel**.. Esc

If you accept the change, Excel inserts the value it
determined into the cell that was used for the
unknown value.

Formula—Protecting

*See "Cells—Protecting" and "Workbook—Protect-
ing."*

Formula—Setting
Calculation Options

*Specifies how and when formulas will be recalcu-
lated in a workbook or chart.*

1. Open the Tools menu .... Alt + T

2. Select **Options** .... O

3. Select the Calculation tab .... Ctrl + Tab

4. Select a calculation method:

Option	Description
Automatic	Recalculates formulas automatically when a change occurs in a workbook. This is the default choice.
Automatic Except Tables	Recalculates formulas automatically except for tables (which take longer to calculate).
Manual	Allows you to calculate formulas manually, by pressing F9.
Recalculate Before Save	Recalculates formulas automatically every time a workbook is saved.

5. Select your desired workbook options:

Update **R**emote References. Recalculates formulas that refer to data from other applications ....References

Precision as Displayed. Uses the values displayed in cells (as specified by the decimal precision) rather than the actual value in the cell, which can use up to 15 decimal places ....Displayed Uses

1904 **D**ate System. Uses a different date system for date calculations. Instead of measuring from Jan 1, 1900, it measures from Jan 2, 1904 ....Date

Save External **L**ink Values. Saves copies of values that any formulas get from external data sources, thus speeding up the recalculation ....Save

6. Enter an iteration setting to control the number of times Excel recalculates a formula during goal seeking.

7. When you are done, select **OK** ....⏎

TIP

If you set the calculation method to manual, you can recalculate a workbook by returning to the **Options dialog box/ Calculation** tab, and clicking on Calc **N**ow or Calc **S**heet. The Calc **N**ow button recalculates the entire workbook. Calc **S**heet recalculates only the active worksheet. A faster way to recalculate is to press **F9** for Calc Now or **Shift+F9** for Calc Sheet.

Formula—Scenarios

See "Scenarios—Creating" and "Scenarios—Viewing."

Formula—Solver

Solves a formula for a maximum, minimum, or specified result. Solver is used to determine two or more unknown values. To determine a single unknown value, see "Formula—Goal Seeking."

EXAMPLE

You have a toy factory that makes three toys: clowns, fire engines, and talking robots. You need to sell $70,000 worth of toys per year just to break even. You want a general idea of how many of each toy you have to sell (and make), in order to determine some production goals. Your cells might contain the following data:

A1 ....$5.00 (Gross from one clown)

A2 ....$8.00 (Gross from one fire engine)

A3 ....$12.00 (Gross from one talking robot)

B1 ....0 (No entry—Solver will determine)

B2 ....0 (No entry—Solver will determine)

B3 ....0 (No entry—Solver will determine)

C1 ....=A1*B1

C2 ....=A2*B2

C3 ....=A3*B3

C4 ....=SUM(C1:C3)

You then tell Solver to make the result in C4 to equal **70000** by playing with the values in cells B1, B2, and B3.

1. Select the cell that you
    want to set a goal for. (In the
    example, this would be cell **C4**.)

2. Open the **T**ools menu .... Alt + T
    and select Solver   V

3. Select one of the following options:

    Max increases the goal cell value
    to the largest possible value (used
    mostly in mathematical or scientific
    models) .... Alt + M

    Min decreases the goal cell
    value to the smallest possible
    value (used mostly in mathematical
    or scientific models) .... Alt + N

    Value sets the goal cell value
    to the value you specify in the
    Value of text box .... Alt + V

4. If you selected **V**alue, enter the
    desired target value .... *value*

5. In the **B**y Changing Cells box,
    enter the cells to adjust
    to reach the desired solution.
    (In the example, this would
    be cells **B1:B3**.) .... Alt + B
                                                        ↑ or ↓

You can drag over the cells with your
mouse in order to enter the desired
range.

MOUSE

6. **(Optional)** Specify any
   constraints to specific cells
   by selecting the **A**dd button .... <kbd>Alt</kbd>+<kbd>A</kbd>

EXAMPLE Say you knew you could sell 1500 clowns
and 2000 fire engines, and you want to
know how many talking robots you
needed to sell to make up the difference.
You could add constraints that tell Solver
to set B1 equal to (=) **1500** and B2 equal
to **2000**.

7. Select the **S**olve button. .... <kbd>Alt</kbd>+<kbd>S</kbd>

8. To save the changes, choose
   Keep Solver Solution, and
   select **OK** .... <kbd>Alt</kbd>+<kbd>K</kbd>
   <kbd>↵</kbd>

   OR

   To cancel the changes, choose
   Restore **O**riginal Values, and
   select **OK** .... <kbd>Alt</kbd>+<kbd>O</kbd>
   <kbd>↵</kbd>

When the Solver Results dialog box appears, you
can save your solver specifications as a scenario and
use it later. For more information on creating and
using scenarios, see *"Scenarios—Creating."*

Formula—Totals

See "Data List—Subtotals" and "AutoSum."

Formula—Using Named Cells and Ranges

References cells and cell ranges by name, rather than by using cell addresses. For information on naming cells and ranges, see "Names—Defining Cell and Range Names."

EXAMPLE You want to enter a formula that subtracts the expenses in cell Sheet2!K34 (named **Expenses**) from the income in cell Sheet1!L45 (named **Income**). Instead of entering the formula as =Sheet1!L45-Sheet2!K34, you can enter the formula as =**Income–Expenses**.

1. Select the cell in which you want to insert the formula.

2. Begin typing the formula until you need to refer to a named cell or range.

3. Open the Insert menu .... `Alt`+`I`

4. Choose **Name** .... `N`

5. Select **Paste** .... `P`

6. Go to the Paste **Name** list .... `Alt`+`N`

7. Select the name to paste into the formula .... `↑` or `↓`

8. Select **OK** .... `↵`

TIP

If you know the names you want to use in your formula, you don't have to select them from a list. Simply type the names. Don't forget to type the mathematical operators.

Formula—Viewing in Cells

Displays formulas, rather than results, in the cells.

1. Open the Tools menu .... $\boxed{\text{Alt}}$+$\boxed{\text{T}}$

2. Select Options .... $\boxed{\text{O}}$

3. Select the View tab .... $\boxed{\text{Ctrl}}$+$\boxed{\text{Tab}}$

4. Select Formulas .... $\boxed{\text{Alt}}$+$\boxed{\text{R}}$

5. Select OK .... $\boxed{\leftarrow}$

TIP

To "toggle" the display from formulas to results and back, press **Ctrl+'**. That's Ctrl plus the accent key (') not the apostrophe (').

Functions—Inserting with the Function Wizard

Leads you through the process of inserting an Excel function into a cell. You can use functions alone, or as part of a formula.

EXAMPLE

A function is a predefined formula that performs simple or complex calculations. For example, the function SUM can total a range of numbers; AVERAGE averages a range; and PMT can determine the payment you would have on a loan given the principal, interest rate, and number of payment periods.

1. Select the cell to hold the formula or function. Begin typing the formula if necessary.

2. Open the **I**nsert menu .... `Alt`+`I`

3. Choose Function .... `F`

TIP

To bypass the Insert menu, click on the **Function Wizard** button (the button with the **fx** on it) in the **Standard** toolbar.

4. Go to the Function **C**ategory box .... `Alt`+`C`

5. Select the desired function type .... `↑` or `↓`

6. Go to the Function **N**ame list .... `Alt`+`N`

7. Select the desired function .... `↑` or `↓`

8. Select the Next >button .... `↵`

9. In the text boxes, type the addresses of the cells whose values you want to use in the function's argument. (You can type addresses or drag over the cells with the mouse.)

TIP

Whenever you click inside a text box, the Function Wizard displays a description of the item, telling you what the abbreviation stands for and the purpose of the entry in the function argument.

EXAMPLE

If you are using the AVERAGE function, select the cells whose values you want to average. If you are using the PMT function, select the cells that have the interest (rate), principle (pv or present value), number of payment periods (nper), and future value (0).

11. Select the Finish button .... Alt + F

To edit an existing function, select the cell that contains the function, but do not double-click on the cell or press F2 to enter Edit mode. Then, click on the **Function Wizard** button.

Go To

See "Cells—Go To."

Graphic Objects—Bringing to Front

Brings an object from the background to the foreground, in front of all other overlapping objects. See also, "Graphic Objects—Sending to Back."

1. Click on the border of the object you want to bring to front.

2. Open the Format menu, and select **P**lacement.

3. Select **B**ring to Front.

MOUSE

To bypass the Format menu, right-click on the border of the object and select Bring to Front. If the Drawing toolbar is displayed, click on the object and then click on the **Bring to Front** button.

Graphic Objects—Copying

Copies a graphic object, and places the copy where specified. You can copy objects just as you copy data (see "Data—Copying"). A quicker way is to use the Drag and Drop feature:

1. Move the mouse pointer over the border of the graphic object you want to copy.

2. Hold the **Ctrl** key and drag the object to where you want it.

3. Release the mouse button.

Graphic Objects—Creating

Places graphic objects, including arrows, lines, rectangles, ovals, circles, and text boxes, on a worksheet.

TIP

To draw objects, you use the Drawing toolbar. To turn it on, select **View** Toolbars, click on **Drawing**, and select **OK**. For more information about toolbars, see *"Toobars—Showing and Hiding"* and *"Toolbars—Selecting a Tool."*

1. Click on the button for the object you want to draw.

2. Move the mouse pointer to where you want the upper left corner of the object placed.

3. Hold down the mouse button and drag the pointer until the object is the desired size and shape.

4. Release the mouse button. (If you selected the FreeForm tool, you can click with the mouse to create a drawing consisting of several lines.)

5. If you selected the **Freeform** button, double-click to stop drawing.

TIP

Tips for drawing objects:

- To draw several objects of the same shape, double-click on the tool. Click on a different tool to stop.

- To draw a uniform object (a perfect circle or square), hold down the **Shift** key while dragging.

- To align an object with the worksheet grid, hold down the **Alt** key while dragging.

Graphic Objects—Deleting

Deletes a graphic object from a worksheet.

1. Right-click on the border of the object you want to delete.

> To delete more than one graphic object at a time, hold down the **Shift** key while left-clicking on each object. Then, right-click on any of the selected objects.

2. Select **Clear** or press .... Delete

Graphic Objects—Drawing Toolbar

See "Toolbars—Showing and Hiding."

Graphic Objects—Formatting

Modifies the appearance of a graphic object, including the object's line thickness, line color, shading, alignment, and font (for text boxes).

1. Click on the border of the object(s) you want to format.

TIP

To format several objects, hold down the
Shift key while clicking on each object.

2. Open the Format menu
   and select Object .... Ctrl + 1

MOUSE

Right-click on one of the selected objects,
and choose **Format Object**.

3. Click on the tab for
   the type of formatting
   you want to change .... Ctrl + Tab

   Patterns lets you change the line thickness
   and color (border) and the shading (fill) for
   the object.

   Protection lets you prevent the object from
   being changed by someone else. (See also,
   "Workbook—Protecting.")

   Properties lets you specify whether or not
   you want the object sized when you resize
   your cells.

   Font lets you specify a type size, style, and
   attributes for text in a text box.

Alignment lets you set the vertical and horizontal position of text inside an object.

4. Enter the desired
   formatting settings .... Alt +*selection letter*

5. Repeat steps 3 and 4 for
   each type of formatting you
   want to change.

6. Select the **OK** button .... ↵

Graphic Objects—Grouping and Ungrouping

Groups several graphic objects together, to treat them as a single object to move, size, or format.

1. Hold down the **Shift** key and click on the border of every object you want to include in the group.

2. Click on the **Group Objects** button in the **Drawing** toolbar.

TIP

If the objects you want to group neighbor each other, click on the **Drawing Selection** button, and use the mouse to draw a selection box around the objects. When you release the mouse button, all objects are selected.

To ungroup objects:

1. Click on any object in the group.

2. Click on the **Ungroup Objects** button in the
    Drawing toolbar.

Graphic Objects—Inserting Pictures

*Inserts a scanned image, clip-art file, or other
graphic object into an Excel worksheet.*

1. Select the cell where you
    want the upper left corner
    of the picture placed.

2. Open the Insert menu .... Alt + I

3. Choose **Picture** .... P

4. Change to the drive and
    directory that contains your
    clip-art or graphics files.

5. Go to the File **Name** list .... Alt + N

6. Select the name of the graphics
    file to insert .... ↑ ↓

7. Select the **OK** button.............................. ↵

Graphic Objects—Moving

Moves a graphic object to a new location.

1. Move the mouse pointer over the border of
    the object you want to move.

To move several objects together, hold down the **Shift** key while clicking on each object's border. Then move the mouse pointer over the border of any selected object.

2. Hold down the mouse button and drag the graphic object to where you want it.

3. Release the mouse button.

Graphic Objects—Selecting

Displays handles around object(s); you can size, move, format, copy, or delete.

1. Position the mouse pointer over the border of the object you want to select.

Some objects (such as hollow shapes) require you to click on a border. Other objects (such as charts, clip-art drawings, filled shapes, and text boxes) allow you to click anywhere inside the object. When selecting an object, just make sure the mouse pointer looks like an arrow, not a plus sign (+), before you click.

2. Click the mouse button.

To select multiple objects, hold down the **Shift** key while clicking on each object. You can also select multiple objects by clicking on the **Drawing Selection** button in the **Drawing** toolbar, and using the mouse to draw a selection box around the objects.

Graphic Objects—Sending to Back

Sends a graphic object to the back, behind all other objects.

1. Click on the border of the object you want to send to the back.

2. Open the Format menu.

3. Select **P**lacement.

4. Select **S**end to Back.

TIP

To bypass the Format menu, right-click on the border of the object and select **Send to Back**. If the Drawing toolbar is displayed, click on the object, and then click on the **Send to Back** button.

Graphic Objects—Sizing and Shaping

Changes the size or dimensions of a picture, drawing, or chart.

1. Click on the border of the object you want to resize.

TIP

To change the size or shape of several objects at once, hold down the **Shift** key while selecting each object.

2. Move the mouse pointer over one of the selection handles (the small black boxes that surround the selected object). To change one dimension, use a side, top or bottom handle. To change two dimensions, use a corner handle.

3. Hold down the mouse button while dragging the handle.

4. Release the mouse button.

TIP

To change the size of an object but retain its relative dimensions, hold down the **Shift** key while dragging.

Help—Getting Help

Displays a window that contains information about using Excel.

1. Open the Help menu .... Alt + H

2. Select the desired Help option:

   Contents displays groups of help topics. Click on a group to see a list of topics in that group.

   Search for Help on displays a dialog box that lets you search for a topic or option by name.

   Index gives alphabetical lists of topics. Select a letter, then scroll through the list for the topic you want.

Quick Preview provides a brief tour of Excel.

Examples and Demos are on-screen tutorials that show how to perform various tasks.

Lotus 1-2-3 or Multiplan provides the specific help you need to make a smooth transition from those programs to Excel.

Technical Support tells you what to do when all else fails, and how to contact Microsoft's technical support.

About Microsoft Excel provides licensing and system information.

Most help windows contain topics or terms for which you can get more information. Click on a solid-underlined topic to display a separate help window for that topic. Click on a dotted-underlined term to view a definition for the term.

TIP To get specific help about an option or dialog box, click on the **Help** button (the button with the arrow and question mark on it) in the **Standard** toolbar, and then click on the option. With the keyboard, highlight the option or display the dialog box, and press **F1**.

Help—TipWizard

See "TipWizard—Using."

Links—Creating

Creates a connection between data on the current worksheet and data on another worksheet, or data in another workbook or Windows application that supports OLE (object linking and embedding) or DDE (Dynamic Data Exchange). For information on embedding objects, see "Embedded Objects—Creating" and "Embedded Objects—Editing."

TIP

Use links when the source data changes frequently, you want those changes reflected in your workbook, and the source data is available on your computer or network. Use embedded objects when the source data rarely changes or you do not want those changes reflected in your workbook, or when the source data is unavailable.

1. Copy the data you want to link to the Windows clipboard.

EXAMPLE

You can copy data from another worksheet or from another workbook. You can also use the Copy command in another Windows application (such as Paintbrush or Microsoft Word) to copy data to the Clipboard.

2. Select the worksheet and cell into which you want to paste the copied data.

3. Open the Edit menu .... Alt + E

4. Select Paste Special .... ⌊S⌋

5. Select Paste Link .... ⌊Alt⌋+⌊L⌋

6. From the **As** list, select the
   format in which you want
   the data pasted.

EXAMPLE

For example, if you are inserting a picture
from Paintbrush, it can be inserted as a
bit-mapped graphic, as a Paintbrush
picture, or as a standard picture.

7. Select **OK** .... ⌊←⌋

Links—Updating

Updates the values in the dependent linked work-
book with those of the source workbook. By default,
Excel automatically updates a workbook that has
links to external data.

EXAMPLE

You linked a workbook with a graphics
file, saved the workbook, and closed it.
Later, you edited the graphics file. You
want the changes you made to the
graphics file to appear in your workbook.

1. Open the File menu .... ⌊Alt⌋+⌊F⌋

2. Select **Open** .... ⌊O⌋

3. Select the workbook whose
   links you want to update.

4. Click on the **OK** button .... ⌊←⌋

5. When the update links dialog
box appears, choose **Yes** .... ⏎

You can change the Link options so Excel does
not automatically update the links when you change
the source. You can also cancel a link, which leaves
the data inside the workbook but breaks the link
between the data and its source.

1. Open the Edit menu .... Alt + E

2. Select Links .... K

3. Go to the Source File list .... Alt + S

4. Select any links whose update
setting you want to change .... ↑ ↓

TIP

To select more than one link, hold down
the **Ctrl** key while clicking on the link. To
select a group of links, click on the first
link, and then hold down the **Shift** key
while clicking on the last link.

5. To change an update setting, select:

Automatic to have Excel update data automatically in the workbook whenever you edit the
source.

Manual to prevent Excel from updating the
links automatically. To update links, click on
the Update Now button.

6. To update links manually, select the Update
Now button.

7. To open a selected source document in the application used to create it, select the **Open** button.

You can open a source document quickly, in the application used to create it, by double-clicking on the object in your workbook.

MOUSE

6. When done, select the **OK** button.

Macro—Adding to a Button

Adds a previously-recorded macro to a button (a small gray box, used by the mouse, displayed anywhere within the worksheet) for easy access. To record a macro, see "Macro—Recording."

To run the macro once it has been added, click on the displayed button.

EXAMPLE

1. Display the **Drawing** toolbar. See *"Toolbars— Showing and Hiding."*

2. Select the **Create Button** tool.

3. Click within the worksheet to place the upper left corner of the button.

4. To create the button, drag downward to the right.

5. Select a macro to assign to the button.

6. Select **OK**.

TIP

You can change the size, font, text, and other properties of your button by selecting it first with the **Drawing Selection** tool on the **Drawing** toolbar. To change the button's size, drag one of its borders. To change its text, select the text and type. To change other properties, open the Format menu and select Object.

Macro—Adding to a Toolbar

Adds a previously-recorded macro to a toolbar for easy access. To record a macro, see "Macro—Recording."

To run the macro once it has been added, be sure that the toolbar containing the macro is displayed, then click on the macro's button. (See *"Toolbars—Showing and Hiding."*)

1. Display the toolbar to which you wish to add the macro button. See *"Toolbars—Showing and Hiding."*

2. While pointing to the toolbar, click the right mouse button to display the shortcut menu. Select **Customize**.

3. **(Optional)** Add a *custom button* to the displayed toolbar by:

   Selecting the **Custom** category
   Clicking on a button
   And dragging it to a toolbar.

Use a custom button instead of a standard
button when assigning macros, to avoid
overwriting existing functions.

EXAMPLE

4. **(Optional)** To add an existing macro to a
   button already in use on a toolbar:

   Click on the button to which you wish to
   assign a macro ....Open the Tools menu.
   Select **Assign** Macro.

5. Choose a macro to assign to the toolbar
   button.

6. Select **OK**.

Macro—Adding to the Tools Menu

*Adds a previously-recorded macro to the Tools
menu for easy access. To record a macro, see
"Macro—Recording."*

To run the macro once it has been added,
open the Tools menu and select it.

EXAMPLE

1. Open the Tools menu .... Alt + T

2. Select **M**acro .... M

3. Select a macro to add from the
   Macro Name/Reference
   list box .... Alt + M
   ↑ ↓

4. Choose Options .... Alt + O

5. Select Menu Item on Tools Menu .... Alt + U

6. Add a name for the menu command .... Tab
   menuname

> **TIP** To add an underlined shortcut key to the
> menu command, insert **&** in front of the
> appropriate letter. For example, if you type
> **&Company Name**, the command Company
> Name will appear on the Tools menu.

7. Select **OK** .... ↵

8. Select Close .... Esc

Macro—Pausing Recording

*Pauses the recording of a macro. (To restart record-
ing, see "Macro—Resuming Recording.")*

1. Open the Tools menu .... Alt + T

2. Select Record Macro .... R

3. Select Stop Recording .... S

Instead of steps 1 and 2, click on the **Stop Macro** button.

MOUSE

Macro—Recording

Records frequently-used keystrokes or Excel commands, and saves them as a macro.

EXAMPLE

For example, if you enter your name or your company's name often, create a macro to enter it for you very quickly with no mistakes. Then you can run the macro by pressing a couple of keys.

TIP

When you record a macro, *absolute references* (actual cell addresses) are used by default. To record *relative cell references* (references to the relationship between cells recorded in the macro), open the Tools menu, select Record Macro, then select Use Relative References. Then record the macro.

TIP

If you record your macro using relative references (as explained in the previous tip), all additional macros will be recorded that way. To turn off the option, again open the Tools menu and select Record Macro, then select Use Relative References.

1. Open the Tools menu ....`Alt`+`T`
2. Select Record Macro ....`R`
3. Select Record New Macro ....`R`

Instead of steps 1 to 3, click on the **Record Macro** button on the **Visual Basic** toolbar.

MOUSE

4. Go to the Macro Name box.................`Alt`+`M`
5. Enter a name for the macro ....*name*

For example, enter *CompanyName*.

EXAMPLE

5. **(Optional)** Change additional
   Options ....`Alt`+`O`

   Menu Item on Tools Menu
   Add macro as a command
   on the Tools menu ....`Alt`+`U`

   Shortcut Key   Add a key
   combination for starting
   the macro ....`Alt`+`K`
   letter

TIP

To run a macro, press the **Ctrl** key simultaneously with the shortcut key you assigned to the macro.

Personal Macro Workbook
Makes macro available in every
workbook by storing it in the
"global workbook" .... Alt + P

This Workbook Makes macro
available whenever this
workbook is open .... Alt + W

New Workbook Stores macro
in a new workbook, which you
can use to store macros
if you want .... Alt + N

Visual Basic Saves as a standard
Excel 5 macro .... Alt + V

MS Excel 4.0 macro Saves as a
macro compatible with Excel 4.0 .... Alt + E

6. To begin recording, choose **OK** .... ⏎

7. Perform the actions or keystrokes
    you want to record.

8. To stop recording, open the
   Tools menu .... **Alt** + **T**

9. Select Stop Recording .... **S**

Instead of steps 8 and 9, click on the **Stop Macro**
button.

Macro—Resuming Recording

*Resumes the recording of a macro that has been
paused.*

TIP

This command records additional keystrokes
and commands, and adds them at the end of
the most recent macro.

1. Open the Tools menu .... **Alt** + **T**

2. Select Record Macro .... **R**

3. Select Record at Mark.................................. **E**

4. Resume executing commands and
   keystrokes for the macro you
   want to record.

Macro—Running

Performs the keystrokes or commands stored in a macro.

1. Open the Tools menu .... $\boxed{Alt}$ + $\boxed{T}$

2. Select Macro .... $\boxed{M}$

3. Go to the Macro Name/Reference
   list box .... $\boxed{Alt}$ + $\boxed{M}$

4. Select a macro to run .... $\boxed{↑}$ or $\boxed{↓}$

5. Select Run .... $\boxed{↵}$

TIP

To run a macro quickly, press the shortcut keys assigned to the macro during recording (for example, **Ctrl+C**).

MOUSE

Instead of steps 1 and 2, click on the **Run Macro** button on the **Visual Basic** toolbar.

TIP

You can interrupt a running macro by pressing **Esc**. To resume an interrupted macro, select **Continue** by clicking on it (or pressing **Alt+C**). To cancel the macro, select End by clicking on it (or pressing **Alt+E**).

Margins—Changing

See "Page Setup—Margins."

Menu Commands—Selecting

Chooses commands from pull-down menus.

Mouse Steps

1. Click on a menu to open it.

2. Click on a command to select it from an open menu.

Many commands have corresponding toolbar buttons for easier access. For example, to select the **F**ile **O**pen command, simply click on the **File Open** button located on the **Standard** toolbar.

Often-used commands are a click away through a *shortcut menu*. To get a shortcut menu, move the mouse pointer over the object you wish to affect (for example, a cell, toolbar, or chart), and click the right mouse button. The shortcut menu opens; to select a command, click on it.

Keyboard Steps

1. Press and hold .... **Alt**

2. Type the underlined
   letter of the menu
   you wish to open .... ***underlined letter***

   OR

   Highlight the menu .... ← or →
   And press .... ↵

3. Type the underlined letter
   of the command you
   wish to select .... ***underlined letter***

   OR

   Highlight the command .... ↑ or ↓
   And press   ↵

TIP

Many commands have *shortcut keys*
displayed next to their names on the
menu (for example, shortcut **Ctrl+O** next
to the **F**ile **O**pen command). To select a
command without opening a menu, press
its shortcut key combination (in this case,
the **Ctrl** key, plus the letter **O**), then
release.

Microsoft Query—Creating a Data Source

Creates a new data source to be used in creating a
query. A data source identifies the directory (and

the files) which contain the data to be used in a query.

1. From the Select Data Source dialog box, choose **Other**.

2. Select **New**.

3. Select a file type.

4. Select **OK**.

5. Enter a data source name.

EXAMPLE

For example, type **Personnel Database**.

6. Enter a description.

EXAMPLE

For example, **Names and Addresses of Active Employees**.

7. Select a source directory:

   Choose Select Directory.
   Select a directory from those listed.
   Select **OK**.

   OR

   Select **U**se Current Directory.

8. **(Optional)** Select **O**ptions and change desired options, such as the number of rows to scan.

9. Select **OK**.

Microsoft Query—Creating a Query

Extracts data from external databases (such as Microsoft Access, Paradox, dBASE 3 and 4, and Microsoft FoxPro), or other Excel workbooks. You can also combine, select and sort data from several sources.

TIP

Microsoft Query is an *add-in* that must be installed before using it. If you selected *full installation* when installing Excel, Microsoft Query has been installed for you. If needed, rerun Microsoft Excel Setup to install Microsoft Query before proceeding.

TIP

Once it is installed, you must activate Microsoft Query from within Excel before using it. See *"Add-ins—Making Add-ins Available."*

1. Open a new workbook to contain the results of your query.

2. Open the **Data** menu.

3. Select Get External Data.

4. Choose a data source from the Available Data Source List.

If you want to extract data from a source
that isn't listed, or if you often extract data
from the same source, you may want to
create a new data source all your own. See
*"Microsoft Query—Creating a Data
Source."*

5. Select Use.

6. Add data tables (database/datalist
   files) to those available for
   your query:

   Select a database/datalist file to add.
   Select **Add**.
   Repeat these two steps to add
   additional database/datalist files.
   Select **Close**.

You can add additional tables (database/
datalist files) to your query later with the
Table **Add** command.

7. Select the fields you want to extract
   from the database/datalist files
   to your Excel workbook:

   Double-click on any field.

   OR

   Drag a field from a table pane to the
   data pane at the bottom of the screen.

OR

Select a field from the data pane's
drop-down list box.

8. **(Optional)** Delete unwanted fields
   from the data pane by selecting
   them and pressing ....

9. **(Optional)** Rearrange fields within
   the data pane by dragging them
   to the desired location.

10. **(Optional)** Select the records to
    extract. See *"Microsoft Query—
    Selecting Specific Records
    to Extract."*

11. Open the File menu.

12. Select Return Data to
    Microsoft Excel.

Instead of steps 11 and 12, click the
Return Data to Excel button on the
Query and Pivot toolbar.

MOUSE

13. **(Optional**) Select an option in the
    Get External Data dialog box:

    Keep Query Definition   Stores the query
    definition within the workbook file.

Include Field Names   Places field names (column headings) at the top of the extracted data.

Include Row Numbers   Places a row number (record number) in the first column of the extracted data.

Destination   Selects the location (within a worksheet) for the extracted data.

14. Select **OK**.

Microsoft Query—Selecting Specific Records to Extract

Identifies the records to extract from a database/ datalist file.

For example, use this command to select only active employees from a personnel database.

EXAMPLE

1. From within Microsoft Query, open the Criteria menu.

2. Select **A**dd Criteria.

3. Select a Field from the drop-down list box.

For example, select *Employee Status*.

EXAMPLE

4. Select a comparision Operator.

For example, select *equals*.

EXAMPLE

5. Select a value:

   Enter a value in the **Value** text box.

   OR

   Select **Values**.
   Select a value from those listed.
   Select **OK**.

6. **(Optional)** Select a **Total** for comparision.

7. Select **Add**.

8. Repeat steps 3 to 7 to add additional selection criteria, selecting either **And** or **Or** between criteria.

You can also add additional criteria at a later time with the **Criteria Add Criteria** command.

TIP

9. Select **Close**.

TIP

To edit a selection criterion, double-click on it and then make your changes from the dialog box. To delete a criterion, select it and press **Delete**. To remove all selection criteria, open the **Criteria** menu and select **R**emove All Criteria.

Names—Applying Cell and Range Names

Searches the cells in a selected range for formulas, and replaces the cell references with names. To name cells or ranges, refer to "Names—Defining Cell and Range Names."

1. Select the cells that contain the formulas whose cell addresses you want to change into names.

2. Open the **I**nsert menu .... `Alt`+`I`

3. Select **N**ames .... `N`

4. Select **A**pply .... `A`

5. In the Apply **N**ames list, select the names to apply .... `Alt`+`N`

    `↑` or `↓`

    `Space`

6. **(Optional)** To replace all cell references (relative or absolute), select the **I**gnore Relative/ Absolute check box .... `Alt`+`I`

7. **(Optional)** To replace the cell reference with row and column names, select the Use Row and Column Names check box .... `Alt`+`U`

8. Select **OK** .... `↵`

Names—Creating From Labels

Creates a name for a cell from its contents.

EXAMPLE

For example, if a cell contains a label such as **April '93**, then the name APRIL_93 is created.

1. Select the cell(s) you want to name.

2. Open the Insert menu .... `Alt`+`I`

3. Select **Name** .... `N`

4. Select **Create** .... `C`

TIP

To create a name quickly, press **Ctrl+Shift+F3**.

5. Select an option.
    Top Row .... `Alt`+`T`
    Left Column .... `Alt`+`L`
    Bottom Row .... `Alt`+`B`
    Right Column .... `Alt`+`R`

6. Select **OK** ....

TIP

You can edit names later. Open the Insert menu, select Names, and select Define. Choose the name you want to edit, and type a new name.

Names—Defining Cell and Range Names

Defines a name for the selected cell or range. This name can then be used to refer to cells in formulas and in dialog boxes when you need to specify a cell or range. To create a name based on a cell's contents, see "Names—Creating From Labels." For more information about using cell and range names in formulas, see "Formula—Using Named Cells and Ranges."

1. Select the cell(s) you want to name.

2. Open the Insert menu .... **Alt**+**I**

3. Select **Name** .... **N**

4. Select **Define** .... **A**

TIP

To define a name quickly, press **Ctrl+F3**.

5. Type the name you want to use ....*name*

6. Select the **Add** button .... **Alt**+**A**

The Define Name dialog box stays open, so you can define additional cells and ranges. Type a name in the Names in **Workbook** text box; go to the **Refers to** text box; type the desired range or drag over it in the worksheet.

7. Select **OK** ....

Select the cell or range you want to name, click inside the name text box (left side of the formula bar), and type the name you want to use. Press **Enter**.

You can edit names later. Open the **Insert** menu, select **Names**, and select **Define**. Choose the name you want to edit, and type a new name.

New File

See "Workbook—New."

New Workbook

See "Workbook—New."

Number—Formatting

See "Cells—Changing the Appearance of Numbers."

OLE (Object Linking and Embedding)

See "Links—Creating" and "Embedded Objects—Creating."

Open File

See "Workbook—Opening."

Open Workbook

See "Workbook—Opening."

Orientation

See "Page Setup—Page Size and Orientation."

Outline—Creating

Creates an outline from data in a range or worksheet. If you are using a data list, you can summarize data and create subtotals with the outlining feature. See "Data List—Subtotals."

Once your outline is created, you can easily control the level of detail displayed. See "Outline—Displaying and Hiding Detail." To remove an outline, see "Outline—Removing."

EXAMPLE

For example, use this command to hide detail rows while you analyze subtotals in a large spreadsheet.

1. Select a range to outline..

TIP

To outline the entire worksheet, select
only one cell in the worksheet.

2. Open the Data menu .... **Alt**+**D**
3. Select Group and Outline .... **G**
4. Select Auto Outline .... **A**

TIP

You can create your own outline groups
by selecting related cells and opening the
Data menu, selecting Group and Outline,
and then selecting Group.

Outline—Displaying and Hiding Detail

*When Excel creates an outline, it displays outline
symbols to the left of each row, and/or at the top of
each column. You can use these symbols to hide or
display detail:*

1 2 3 The number buttons (at the top
of the outline area) control the detail for the
entire list. Click on **1** to see the least detail or
3 to see the most detail.

– Click on a minus button to see less detail.

+ Plus signs appear when you click on a
minus button to see less detail. To see more
detail, click on a plus button.

Outline—Removing

Removes an outline.

1. Open the **D**ata menu .... Alt + D
2. Select **G**roup and Outline .... G
3. Select **C**lear Outline C

Page Breaks—Automatic

Displays or hides the location of page breaks that Excel inserts according to page size and margins. To change the page size setting, see "Page Setup—Page Size and Orientation." To change margins, see "Page Setup—Margins." By default, Excel displays automatic page breaks.

1. Open the **T**ools menu .... Alt + T
2. select **O**ptions .... O
3. Click on the **View** tab .... Control + Tab
4. Select **Au**tomatic Page Breaks .... Alt + U
5. Select the **OK** button .... ↵

Page Breaks—Inserting and Removing

Inserts a manual page break (horizontal or vertical or both) and displays it as a dashed line.

1. Select the cell below and to the right of where you want to insert the page break.

TIP To insert only a horizontal page break, select a cell in column A that is just below where you want the break. To insert only a vertical break, select a cell in row 1 that is just to the right of where you want the break.

2. Open the Insert menu .... Alt + I

3. Select Page **B**reak .... B

TIP To delete a page break, select the cell below or to the right of the page break, open the Insert menu, and select Remove page **B**reak.

Page Setup—Headers and Footers

Adds text to the top or bottom of every printed page.

1. Open the File menu .... Alt + F

2. Select Page Set**u**p .... U

3. Go to the **Header/Footer** tab .... Control + Tab

4. Select a header from the Header list .... Alt + A ↓

OR

Select **C**ustom Header, and type your own header. You can use the buttons to insert

today's date and time, and to insert page
numbers and names.

5. Select a footer from
   the Footer list .... `Alt` + `F`
                                                              `↓`

   OR

   Select Custom Footer, and type your own
   footer. You can use the buttons to insert
   today's date and time, and to insert page
   numbers and names.

6. Select **OK** .... `⏎`

Page Setup—Margins

*Sets the top, bottom, left, and right margins for a
printed page.*

1. Open the File menu .... `Alt` + `F`
2. Select Page Setup .... `U`
3. Go to the **Margins** tab .... `Control` + `Tab`
4. Select the margin you
   want to change:

   Top .... `Alt` + `T`

   Bottom .... `Alt` + `B`

   Left .... `Alt` + `L`

   Right .... `Alt` + `R`

5. Type the desired
   setting (in inches) ....*number*

MOUSE To change a setting with the mouse, click
on the up or down arrow to the right of
the setting's text box. This increases or
decreases the setting by .25" (a quarter of
an inch).

6. Repeat steps 4 and 5 for
   each margin you want to change.

7. **(Optional)** Specify the
   distance you want the
   header or footer from the
   edge of the page:

   Header to specify the distance
   of the header from the top
   edge of the page ....⎡Alt⎤+⎡A⎤

   Footer to specify the distance
   of the footer from the bottom
   edge of the page ....⎡Alt⎤+⎡F⎤

8. **(Optional)** To center text
   on the page, choose:

   Horizontally centers the text between the left
   and right margins.

   Vertically centers the text between the top and
   bottom margins.

9. Select **OK** ....⎡↵⎤

Page Setup—Page Size and Orientation

Specifies the paper size you intend to print on, the position of the printing on a page, and the desired print quality.

1. Open the File menu .... `Alt`+`F`
2. Select Page Setup .... `U`
3. Go to the **Page** tab .... `Control`+`Tab`
4. Select a page orientation:

   Portrait prints normally, from left to right across a page .... `Alt`+`T`

   Landscape prints sideways on a page, making the page wider than it is tall .... `Alt`+`L`

5. **(Optional)** Select a scaling percent:

   Adjust to lets you increase or decrease the size of print by a specific percent from 10% to 400% .... `Alt`+`A`

   Fit to automatically decreases the print size as necessary to fit the worksheet on the specified number of pages .... `Alt`+`F`

6. Open the Paper Size list .... `Alt`+`Z`

7. Select the size of the paper
   on which you are printing .... ⬇️

8. Open the Print **Q**uality list .... Alt + Q

9. Select the desired print resolution.

10. (**Optional**) Select First
    Page Number .... Alt + R

11. Type the number with which
    you want to start numbering
    pages (usually 1) .... *number*

12. Select **OK** .... ⏎

Page Setup—Sheet Preferences

*Specifies which areas of a workbook to print; lets
you enter titles and control the page order; and
controls whether gridlines, row and column headings, and cell notes get printed. If you do not specify
sheet preferences, Excel prints every part of the
workbook that contains data, and includes
gridlines.*

1. Open the File menu .... Alt + F

2. Select Page Set**u**p .... U

3. Go to the **Sheet** tab .... Control + Tab

4. Select Print **A**rea .... Alt + A

5. Type the range(s) of cells you
   want to print. To print more
   than one range, type a comma
   between ranges.

MOUSE

Drag over the range with your mouse. To select more than one range, hold down the **Ctrl** key while dragging over each additional range.

6. **(Optional)** Select a **Print Titles** option:

   Rows to Repeat at Top to print a specific row at the top of every page .... Alt + R

   Columns to Repeat at Left to print a specific column at the left on every page .... Alt + C

7. Select the row or column you want to repeat on every page.

8. Select the items you want to print (an X in the item's check box means it will print):

   Gridlines .... Alt + G

   Notes .... Alt + N

   Draft **Q**uality prints in a lower quality .... Alt + Q

   Black and White prints color items in black and white on a color printer .... Alt + B

   Row and Co**l**umn Headings .... Alt + L

9. If your print area is wider than
   a page, select a page order option:

   Down, then Across prints one set
   of columns at a time from the top
   row to the bottom row.....................⌨Alt+D

   Acro**ss**, then Down prints as
   many rows as will fit on one
   page and then starts printing
   the first row in the next set
   of columns...⌨Alt+S

10. Select **OK**...⏎

Page Size—Setting

See "Page Setup—Page Size and Orientation."

Pictures—Inserting

See "Graphic Objects—Inserting Pictures."

Preview Printing

See "Printing—Print Preview."

Pivot Table—Creating from a Data List

Organizes and summarizes data in a data list so you can rearrange the data to analyze it in different ways. To create a data list, see "Data List—Creating."

1. Select any cell in the
   data list .... ⬆ ⬇ ⬅ ➡

2. Open the **D**ata menu .... Alt + D

3. Select **P**ivot table .... P

> **TIP**
>
> To bypass the Data menu, click on the
> **PivotTable Wizard** button in the **Query
> and Pivot** toolbar. To display this toolbar,
> select View Toolbars, click on **Query and
> Pivot**, and click on **OK**.

4. Select **M**icrosoft Excel
   List or Database .... Alt + M

5. Select the **Next** button .... ⏎

6. Type the cell addresses that
   define the range of cells that
   contain the data you want to use .... *range*

> **MOUSE**
>
> You can drag over the range with the
> mouse pointer.

7. Click on the **Next** button .... ⏎

8. Drag the buttons on the right
   to where you want the row
   headings, column headings,
   or data to appear:

   Create a drop-down list for the data items. To
   see the data for one item, you select it from
   the list .... **PAGE**

Displays the data items in a row, from left to right ....**ROW**

Displays the data items in a column from top to bottom ....**COLUMN**

Displays summary information for the data, including subtotals and totals ....**DATA**

9. Click on the **Next** button ....

10. Type the address of the cell you want to use for the upper left corner of the table ....*address*

MOUSE

If you do not type a cell address, Excel inserts a new worksheet before the current worksheet and places the pivot table on the new worksheet.

11. Click on the **Finish** button ....Alt + F

Pivot Table—Rearranging

Rearranges the rows and columns in a pivot table, so you can analyze the data in different ways.

EXAMPLE

Your pivot table displays sales amounts for several sales people who are listed in columns. You want the sales people listed in rows. You can drag the Salesperson button from the top of the table to the left side to display that data in rows.

1. Drag a data field button where you want it:

   Above the rest of the table to create a page drop-down list for the data items.

   To the left to display the items in a row.

   To the top of the table to display the items in a column.

   Off the table to remove the items. When you drag an item off the table, it appears with a black X through it.

2. Release the mouse button.

TIP You can also rearrange your table by using the PivotTable Wizard. Select one of the cells in the table, and then open the **D**ata menu and select **P**ivot table. This displays the PivotTable Wizard Step 3 of 4 dialog box—the one that has the field buttons. Drag the buttons around to new positions to create the desired arrangement.

Printing—Print Area

See "Page Setup—Sheet Preferences."

Printing—Print Preview

Displays workbook data on-screen as it will appear when printed on paper.

You cannot edit a workbook while previewing it.

1. Go to the workbook you want to preview.

2. Select the worksheet you want to preview.

3. Open the File menu .... `Alt`+`F`

4. Select Print Preview .... `V`

To bypass the File menu, click on the **Print Preview** button in the **Standard** toolbar. It's the button with the magnifying glass on it.

5. Select any of the following options:

   Next displays the next page .... `Alt`+`N`

   Previous displays the
   previous page .... `Alt`+`P`

   Zoom toggles between
   full-page and actual-size
   views .... `Alt`+`Z`

   Print displays the Print
   dialog box to print
   the workbook .... `Alt`+`T`

   Setup displays the Page
   Setup dialog box .... `Alt`+`S`

Margins allows you to adjust
the margins of the document
by dragging the margin
markers .... `Alt`+`M`

Close closes the preview
window and returns
to the document .... `Alt`+`C`

6. When finished previewing,
   select Close .... `Alt`+`C`

Printing—Print Titles

See "Page Setup—Sheet Preferences."

Printing—Workbook

*Prints the active workbook, worksheet, or selected
cells. To control margins, print headers or footers,
or select a page size or orientation, see "Page
Setup."*

1. Activate the workbook and
   worksheet you want to print.

2. To print only certain
   worksheets, select the
   worksheets you want to print.

3. To print only selected cells,
   select the cells you want to print.

4. Open the File menu .... `Alt`+`F`

5. Select **Print** .... P

> TIP
>
> To bypass the **File** menu, press **Ctrl+P**.

Specify what you want to print:

Selection to print
selected cells .... Alt + N

Selected Sheet(s) to print
selected worksheets .... Alt + D

Entire Workbook to print
the entire workbook .... Alt + E

> TIP
>
> Excel prints only the section of the
> workbook or worksheet that contains
> data.

7. To print more than one
copy, select **Copies** and
type the desired number .... Alt + C
                                                number

8. Specify which pages you
want to print:

All to print all pages .... Alt + A

Page(s) to print only specific
pages. Then, enter the pages

you want to print in the **From**
and **To** text boxes .... Alt + G

9. Select **OK** .... ⏎

MOUSE

To print only one copy of the current
worksheet, you can bypass the Print dialog
box by clicking on the Print button in the
Standard toolbar.

Printing—Worksheet

See "Printing—Workbook."

Range—Applying Names

See "Names—Applying Cell and Range Names."

Range—Defining Names

See Names—Defining Cell and Range Names."

Range—Filling Cells

Copies the contents and formatting of one cell in a range and pastes the copy up, down, left, or right into all the other selected cells. See also, "AutoFill."

1. Select the cells you want to fill, including the
   cell which contains the data and formatting
   you want to copy.

TIP

The cell that contains the data and formatting you want to copy should be at top-, bottom-, left-, or rightmost cell of the selection.

2. Open the Edit menu .... Alt + E

3. Select Fill I

4. Select the direction in which you want to fill:

   Down .... D

   Right .... R

   Up .... U

   Left L

TIP

To bypass the Edit menu, press **Ctrl+D** to fill down or **Ctrl+R** to fill right.

TIP

To fill by dragging, select the cell you want to copy. Move the mouse pointer over the fill handle (the tiny box in the lower right corner of the selected cell); the mouse pointer turns into a small, solid plus sign (+). Drag so the border outlines all the cells you want to copy to, then release the mouse button.

Range—Filling with Series

See "Series—Filling Cells with Related Values" and "AutoFill."

Range—Selecting

Defines a rectangular block of cells. (See also "Selecting Cells, Columns, and Rows.") You select ranges to perform an operation on more than one cell at once (for example, to apply formatting or print a range).

1. Type the address of the cell in the upper left corner of the range.

2. Type a colon (:).

3. Type the address of the cell in the lower right corner of the range.

You can often select a range by dragging over the cells with the mouse.

MOUSE

Repeating—Operations and Commands

Repeats the Excel command you just entered.

When Excel cannot repeat a command, the message Can't Repeat appears on the Edit menu.

TIP

1. Perform the Excel command or operation you want to repeat.

2. Open the Edit menu .... $\boxed{Alt}$ + $\boxed{E}$

3. Select **R**epeat .... $\boxed{R}$

TIP
To repeat an operation or command
quickly, press F4 or click on the Repeat
button in the Standard toolbar (the button
with the clockwise arrow on it).

Row—Changing Height

Changes the height of the selected row(s).

1. Select the row(s) whose height
   you want to change.

TIP
To change the row height on the entire
worksheet, press Ctrl+Shift+Spacebar.

2. Open F**o**rmat menu .... $\boxed{Alt}$ + $\boxed{O}$

3. Select **R**ow .... $\boxed{R}$

4. Select H**e**ight .... $\boxed{E}$

5. Type the desired height in points.
   (There are 72 points in an inch.)

6. Select O**K** .... $\boxed{\leftarrow}$

TIP
To have Excel adjust the row height for
you, select the row(s), open the Format
menu, select **R**ow, and select AutoFit.

MOUSE

To adjust row height with a mouse, select the row(s), move the mouse pointer over the bottom border of any of the selected row headings, and drag the border up or down.

Row—Deleting

Removes the selected row from the worksheet and shifts remaining rows up. See also, "Selecting Cells, Columns, and Rows" and "Cells—Deleting."

1. Select any cell in the row you want to delete.

2. Open the Edit menu .... `Alt`+`E`

3. Select **D**elete .... `D`

4. Select Entire **R**ow .... `Alt`+`R`

5. Select **OK** .... `←`

MOUSE

Right-click on the row heading of the row you want to delete, and select Delete from the Shortcut Menu.

Row—Hiding

See "View—Hiding Cells."

Row—Inserting

Inserts an entire row above the currently selected row. See also, "Cells—Inserting."

1. Select the number of rows you want to insert.

TIP

To insert a single row, select any cell in the row. The row will be inserted above the selected row(s).

2. Open the Insert menu ....

3. Select **R**ows ....

MOUSE

To bypass the Insert menu, select the number of rows you want to insert, right-click on one of the rows, and select Insert.

Row—Selecting

See "Selecting Cells, Columns, and Rows."

Save—Workbook, Chart, Slideshow

See "Workbook—Saving."

Scenarios—Creating

Saves various sets of input data so you can play "what-if," by plugging the input data into your model.

EXAMPLE

You created a loan worksheet that calculates a monthly payment amount given the principal, interest, and number of payment periods. You want to play with the principal, interest, and payment period numbers to see what effect various sets of numbers will have on your loan payment. You can create several scenarios that contain different sets of numbers, and then quickly apply a scenario to your model to see what effect it has.

1. Open the Tools menu .... Alt + T

2. Select Scenarios C

3. Select the Add button .... Alt + A

4. Type a name for the scenario .... *text*

5. Go to the Changing Cells box .... Alt + C

6. Type the cell address(es) or range of the cells in your model whose values you want to experiment with .... *range*

MOUSE

You can click on the cells or drag over them with the mouse. To select non-neighboring cells, hold down the Ctrl key while clicking or dragging.

7. Select **OK** ....⏎

8. Type the values you
   want to use for your
   what-if scenario ....*numbers*

9. Select **OK** ....⏎

10. To close the Scenario
    Manager dialog box, select **Close**.

TIP

To edit a scenario, redisplay the Scenario
Manager dialog box, select the scenario
you want to edit, and click on the **Edit**
button.

Scenarios—Viewing

*Applies the numbers you entered in a scenario to
your model, and displays the results.*

1. Open the Tools menu ....`Alt`+`T`

2. Select Scenarios ....`C`

3. Go to the Scenarios list ....`Alt`+`C`

4. Select the scenario you want to use ....`↑` `↓`

5. Select the Show button ....`Alt`+`S`

TIP

You can select a scenario from the
Scenarios drop-down list in the
Workgroup toolbar. To display the
toolbar, open the View menu, select
Toolbars, select **WorkGroup**, and click on
the **OK** button.

Selecting Cells, Columns, and Rows

Selects one or more cells in a worksheet.

Mouse Steps

To Select	Click on
A single cell	The cell.
Range of cells	The cell, and drag over the range.
Entire row	The row heading.
Multiple rows	Drag over the row headings.
Entire column	The column heading.
Multiple columns	Drag over the column headings.
All cells in worksheet	The button at intersection of the row and column headings.
Deselect a cell	Any other cell.

Keyboard Steps

To Select	Press
A single cell	↑ ↓ ← →
Range of cells	Shift + ↑ ↓ ← →
Entire row	Shift + Space
Multiple rows	Shift + Space
	Shift + ↑ ↓

Entire column ....`Control` + `Space`

Multiple columns ....`Control` + `Space`
`Shift` + `←` `→`

All cells in
worksheet ....`Control` + `Shift` + `Space`

Deselect a cell ....`↑` `↓` `←` `→`

TIP

To select cells on more than one worksheet, select the worksheets first. See "Selecting Worksheets."

Selecting Columns

See "Selecting Cells, Columns, and Rows."

Selecting Multiple Ranges of Cells

Select multiple cells, cell ranges, rows or columns in a worksheet.

Mouse Steps

1. Select the first cell, range, row, or column.

2. Hold down the **Ctrl** key while clicking on (or dragging over) the other cells you want to select.

3. Release the Ctrl key and mouse button.

Keyboard Steps

1. Select the first cell, range, row, or column.

2. Press **Shift+F8** ....⟨Shift⟩+⟨F8⟩

3. Use the arrow keys to
   outline cells...............................⟨↑⟩ ⟨↓⟩ ⟨←⟩ ⟨→⟩

4. Press **F8** ....⟨F8⟩

5. Press **Shift+F8** ....⟨Shift⟩+⟨F8⟩

6. Repeat steps 3–5 to select other cells.

Selecting Rows

See *"Selecting Cells, Columns, and Rows."*

Selecting Worksheets

Activates one or more worksheets in a workbook.

To	Do This
Select a single worksheet	Click on the worksheet's tab.
Select neighboring worksheets	Click on the first worksheet in the group, and then hold down the Shift key while clicking on the last worksheet.

| Select non-neighboring worksheets | Hold down the Ctrl key while clicking on the tab for each worksheet. |
| Unselect worksheets | Click on an unselected worksheet. |

TIP

When you select more than one worksheet, the selected worksheets become a group and remain a group until you ungroup them. To ungroup them, click on an unselected worksheet, or hold down the Shift key while clicking on a worksheet in the group.

Series—Creating an AutoFill Series

Lets you create and save a series of items to use with the AutoFill feature. For more information on using AutoFill, see "AutoFill—Copying a Cell's Value."

EXAMPLE

Excel has the days of the week stored as an AutoFill entry. You may want to create AutoFill entries for all the employees in your department or for all the products you sell.

1. Open the Tools menu .... `Alt` + `T`

2. Choose Options .... `O`

3. Go to the **Custom Lists** tab .... `Control` + `Tab`

4. Select the **A**dd button .... Alt + A

5. Type the entries you want
to use for your AutoFill entries.
(Press **Enter** at the end of
each entry.)

EXAMPLE

For example, to create a
list of names, type:

**Mary Joseph Nicholas Alexandra
Anthony Cleopatra**

6. Select **OK** .... ↵

Series—Filling Cells
with Related Values

*Fills a range of selected cells with a series of num-
bers or dates, incrementing the data automatically
as you specify. See also, "AutoFill." The following
table shows some samples:*

Series Type	Initial Entry	Resulting Series
Linear	1,2	3,4,5
	100,99	98,97,96
	1,3	5,7,9
Growth	10 (step 5)	15,20,25
	10 (step 10)	20,30,40
Date	Mon	Tue, Wed, Thur
	Feb	Mar, Apr, May

continues

continued

Series Type	Initial Entry	Resulting Series
	Qtr1	Qtr2, Qtr3, Qtr4
	1992	1993, 1994, 1995
AutoFill	Team 1	Team 2, Team 3, Team 4
	Qtr 4	Qtr 1, Qtr 2, Qtr 3
	1st Quarter	2nd Quarter, 3rd Quarter, 4th Quarter

1. Enter a number or date in the cell where the series is to begin.

2. Select the cells to be filled, including the cell with the number or date.

3. Open the Edit menu .... `Alt`+`E`

4. Select Fill .... `I`

5. Select Series .... `S`

6. Select a **Series in** option:

   Rows—Excel fills across the row .... `Alt`+`R`

   Columns—Excels fills down the column .... `Alt`+`C`

7. Select a series type:

   Linear .... `Alt`+`L`

Growth .... Alt + G

Date .... Alt + D

AutoFill .... Alt + F

8. If you chose **Date**, select
    a date unit:

    Day .... Alt + A

    Weekday .... Alt + W

    Month .... Alt + M

    Year .... Alt + Y

9. Go to the Step Value box .... Alt + S

10. Enter a number to increment
    the set by .... *number*

For example, if you start with 1 and enter a step value of 4, your series will be 1, 5, 9, 13.

EXAMPLE

11. (**Optional**) Go to the
    Stop Value text box .... Alt + O
    Type a value to stop at .... *number*

12. (**Optional**) To create a
    linear or exponential
    growth trend, select **T**rend .... Alt + T

13. Select **OK**.. ⏎

Shortcut Menu

Displays a pop-up shortcut menu when you right-click on a selected cell, a toolbar, or an object. Shortcut menus offer the most commonly used commands for the selected item.

1. Select the desired cell(s) or object.

2. Right-click on the selected cell or object .... **Shift** + **F10**

3. Select a shortcut menu option .... **↑** or **↓**
   ↵

Slide Show—Creating

Lets you create a slide show using worksheets, data lists, charts, and graphics from Excel or other Windows programs. You can run the slide show on your PC monitor, or on another display device that's connected to your computer, but you cannot print a slide show.

1. Open the File menu .... **Alt** + **F**

2. Select New .... **N**

TIP

If the New dialog box does not appear with the Slides option listed, the Slideshow add-in is unavailable. To make it available, see "*Add-Ins—Making Add-Ins Available.*"

3. Select **Slides** .... ⬇

4. Select **OK** .... ↵

5. Use the slide show buttons
   to create your slide show:

   Inserts what you copied to the Clipboard into
   the selected cell as a slide, and displays the
   Edit Slide dialog box .... **Paste Slide**

   Lets you change the display settings of the
   selected slide, including how Excel moves
   from slide to slide and how long a slide is
   displayed on-screen .... **Edit Slide**

   Runs the slide show, displaying slides one
   after another .... **Start Show**

   Displays a dialog box that looks just like the
   Edit Slide dialog box, and lets you enter
   default settings for new slides .... **Set Defaults**

   Deletes the selected rows in the Slideshow
   window and copies them to
   the Clipboard .... **Cut Row**

   Copies the selected rows in the Slideshow
   window to the Clipboard .... **Copy Row**

   Inserts rows from the Clipboard to the row
   above the selected row .... **Paste Row**

Deletes the
selected rows ....**Delete Row**

6. When done creating the slide show, save it.
   For more information, see *"Workbook—
   Saving."*

You can open a slideshow just as you
open an existing workbook. See *"Workbook—Opening."* You can then click on
the **Show** button to run the slide show.

Spelling—Checking

*Checks all of the text in a workbook for misspelled
or unrecognized words, and suggests corrections.*

1. Open the Tools menu .... **Alt**+**T**

2. Select Spelling .... **S**

You can bypass the Tools menu by
pressing **F7** or clicking on the **Spelling**
tool in the **Standard** toolbar (the button
with ABC on it).

3. If the Spelling dialog box appears, displaying
   a questionable word, select one of
   these options:

   Ignore to skip only this
   occurrence of the word ....**Alt**+**I**

Ignore All to ignore every
occurrence of the word .... **Alt** + **G**

Change to replace only
this occurrence of the
word with the word in the
Change To box .... **Alt** + **C**

Change All to replace every
occurrence of the word with
the word in the Change To
box. (To insert an entry in
the Change To box, type
it or select an entry from
the Suggest list.) .... **Alt** + **L**

Add to add the word to
the dictionary, so Excel
will not question it again .... **Alt** + **A**

To close the
Spelling dialog box .... Cancel or Close

Suggest to display a list
of suggested words. You
can select a word from the
list to insert it in the
Change To box .... **Alt** + **S**

Ignore UPPERCASE skips all
words that are in all uppercase
characters, such as acronyms .... **Alt** + **R**

Always Suggest tells Excel
to display possible corrections
in the Suggest list, so you
don't have to click on the
Suggest button .... `Alt`+`Y`

4. When asked if you want to
continue spelling from the
top of the worksheet, select
Yes or **No** .... `Alt`+`Y`

or

`Alt`+`N`

5. When spell checking is
complete, select **OK** .... `↵`

Starting Excel

See "Starting Excel" in the Introduction.

Styles—Applying

*Applies a cell style to the data in the selected cells or
worksheet. Cell styles are named collections of cell,
text, and number formatting that you can apply
together to selected cells. To create your own styles,
see "Styles—Creating."*

1. Select the cell(s) you want to style.

2. Open the **F**ormat menu .... `Alt`+`O`

3. Select **S**tyle .... `S`

4. Go to the Style Name
   drop-down list .... `Alt`+`S`

5. Select a style .... `↑` or `↓`

6. Select **OK** .... `←`

Styles—Creating

Stores cell, text, and number formatting as a group,
so you can apply all the formatting with a single
command.

1. Open the Format menu .... `Alt`+`O`

2. Choose Style. .... `S`

3. Type a name for the style .... ***text***

4. Click on the Add button .... `Alt`+`A`

5. Select any check box
   option to remove the X for
   any attribute you want to
   exclude from the style.

6. Select the Modify button .... `Alt`+`M`

7. Go to the tab for the format
   attribute whose settings you
   want to change .... `Control`+`Tab`

8. Enter your preferences.

9. Repeat steps 7–8 for each attribute whose
   settings you want to change.

10. Select **OK** .... ⏎

11. Select **OK** .... ⏎

TIP

If you have formatted a cell or its contents, you can copy the formatting to create a style. Select the cell, open the Format menu, select **S**tyle, type a name for the style, and click on the **A**dd button.

Subtotals—Summarizing and Analyzing Data

See "Data List—Subtotals."

Summarizing and Analyzing Data

See "Data List—Subtotals" and "Pivot Table— Creating from a Data List."

TipWizard—Turning On and Off

Turns on the Tip Wizard, which displays information on quicker ways to perform the operation you completed.

1. Click on the **TipWizard** button in the Standard toolbar.

2. Use the arrows to the right of the tip to scroll back or forward through the tips.

3. To clear the TipWizard tip list, hold
    down the **Ctrl** key while clicking on the
    TipWizard button again.

Toolbars—Customizing

*Adds or removes buttons from a toolbar. You can
customize an existing toolbar or one you have
created.*

TIP

To create your own toolbar, open the
View menu, select Toolbars, select
Toolbar Name, type a name, and select
New.

1. Open the View menu .... `Alt`+`V`

2. Select Toolbars .... `T`

3. Select Customize .... `C`

4. To move a button, drag it
    from one toolbar to the other.

5. To remove a button from any
    toolbar, drag it off the toolbar.

6. To add a button, select the
    type of item you want to add
    from the **Categories** list.

EXAMPLE

To add tools for applying formats to cells,
select Formatting.

7. Drag the desired button(s) onto a toolbar.

8. Click on the **Close** button when you're done.

Toolbars—Selecting a Button

Selects a button from an Excel toolbar. With some buttons, such as Bold, you first select the cell(s) you want to act upon.

1. Select the cell(s) to change, if necessary.

2. To use a button, click on the button.

3. To use a drop-down list, click on the arrow to the right of the list, and click on the desired item.

4. Complete the operation as you normally would.

TIP

You can move a toolbar to a different portion of the screen by dragging it to a new location. If you drag a toolbar anywhere other than the edge of the Excel program window, it becomes a "floating toolbar" and acts like a window, complete with a title bar and Control menu box.

Toolbars—Showing and Hiding

Displays or hides the following toolbars:

Standard ....contains tools for the most commonly used features.

Formatting ....allows you to quickly assign format including bold and italic type and text alignment.

Query and Pivot ....has tools that let you rearrange pivot tables and work with Microsoft Query.

Chart ....offers tools for creating and manipulating graphs.

Drawing ....contains tools that allow you to draw basic shapes.

TipWizard ....displays the Tip Wizard bar that tells you how to perform tasks more efficiently.

Forms ....has tools for working with forms.

Stop Recording ....contains the stop recording button for macros.

Visual Basic ....has tools for writing programs using Visual Basic.

Auditing ....contains tools for checking the formulas in your worksheets.

WorkGroup ....offers tools for working with Excel on a network.

Microsoft ....contains tools that allow you to work with other Microsoft programs, including Word, Access, FoxPro, and Project.

Full Screen ....displays a button that lets you switch back and forth between full-screen view.

1. Open the View menu ....⎣Alt⎦+⎣V⎦

2. Select Toolbars ....⎣T⎦

3. Select a toolbar to show
   or hide. (An X in the
   toolbar's checkbox means
   it will be displayed.) ....⎣↑⎦ or ⎣↓⎦
   ⎣Space⎦

4. Select **OK**..⎣↵⎦

MOUSE Right-click on any toolbar for a shortcut menu of toolbars and select one to display or hide. Selecting a toolbar from the shortcut menu turns the toolbar on if it is off, or off if it is on.

Toolbars—Tear-Off Palettes

Lets you drag a drop-down palette from a toolbar into the worksheet area to make it more accessible. This works with the Color and Font Color drop-down palettes (on the Formatting toolbar) and similar drop-down palettes.

1. Click on the arrow to the right of the drop down palette.

2. Move the mouse pointer over any part of the palette.

3. Hold down the mouse button and drag the palette to where you want it.

Toolbars—Button Descriptions

See "ToolTips."

ToolTips

Displays the name of a toolbar button or drop-down list whenever you move the mouse pointer over the button.

1. Move the mouse pointer over the desired button or drop-down list.

2. Wait until the ToolTip box appears.

For a brief description of a button use, move the mouse pointer over it and read the note in the status bar. For more detailed information, click on the Help button and then click on the button for which you need help.

TIP

To turn off ToolTips, open the **View** menu, select **T**oolbars, click on the **S**how ToolTips check box, and select **OK**.

TIP

Undo—Commands and Operations

Reverses an Excel command or operation if you made a mistake or changed your mind.

1. Open the Edit menu .... $\boxed{Alt}+\boxed{E}$
2. Select Undo .... $\boxed{U}$

TIP

To undo a command quickly, press **Ctrl+Z** or click on the **Undo** button in the **Standard** toolbar.

View—Changing the Show Options

Changes the way the worksheet appears on-screen. To save selected views and switch between them, see "View Manager".

1. Open the Tools menu .... $\boxed{Alt}+\boxed{T}$
2. Select Options .... $\boxed{O}$
3. Select the **View** tab .... $\boxed{Ctrl}+\boxed{Tab}$
4. **(Optional)** Select Show options:

   Formula Bar   Display or hide the formula bar. .... $\boxed{Alt}+\boxed{F}$

   Status Bar   Display or hide the status bar .... $\boxed{Alt}+\boxed{S}$

Note Indicator   Display or hide
the *flag* (small red dot) indicating
that a note exists for a cell .... `Alt`+`N`

Info **W**indow   Display or hide
the Information Window .... `Alt`+`W`

5. **(Optional)** Select Objects options:

Show **A**ll   Show all objects .... `Alt`+`A`

Show **P**laceholders   Do not display
selected objects, but show where
they are in the worksheet................... `Alt`+`P`

> **TIP**
> Because complex graphic images (which
> take time to present on-screen) are not
> displayed when you choose Show Place-
> holders, you can work faster.

Hi**d**e All   Do not
display objects .... `Alt`+`D`

> **TIP**
> To select Hi**d**e All without opening the
> dialog box, press **Ctrl+6**.

6. **(Optional)** Select Window
Options:

Automatic Page Breaks

Display page breaks .... `Alt`+`U`

Formulas   Display formulas,
and not results .... Alt + R

To select **Formulas** without opening the
dialog box, press **Ctrl+'** (left single
quotation mark).

TIP

Gridlines   Display cell borders .... Alt + G

Color   Select gridline color .... Alt + C

Row & Column Headers
Display the row and
column markers .... Alt + E

Outline Symbols   Display
outline markers .... Alt + O

To select **Outline Symbols** without
opening the dialog box, press **Ctrl+8**.

TIP

Zero Values   Display 0
rather than blank .... Alt + Z

Horizontal Scroll Bar   Display
the horizontal scroll bar .... Alt + T

Vertical Scroll Bar   Display
the vertical scroll bar .... Alt + V

Sheet Tabs   Display the
worksheet markers .... Alt + B

7. Select **OK** .... ⏎

View—Freezing Titles

*Keeps column and/or row titles on-screen while you
scroll through a large worksheet. The worksheet
window is split at the current cell; rows and/or
columns above (or to the left of) the current cell are
frozen. (This does not affect the way a worksheet is
printed.) To split a window into two without freezing rows and/or columns, see "Window—Splitting."
To have titles appear on every page of a printout,
see "Printing—Setting Print Titles."*

1. Move the cursor to the upper left of the
   worksheet area you *do not* wish to freeze.

EXAMPLE

For example, if you wanted to freeze row
headings in column A, and column
headings in rows 1 and 2, move the
cursor to cell **B3**. By choosing cell B3,
rows and columns you want frozen are
located above or to the left of the current
cell (B3).

2. Open the Window menu .... Alt + W

3. Select the Freeze Panes command .... F

TIP

To "unfreeze" your worksheet window
later, open the **Window** command and
select Unfreeze Panes.

TIP

To move between the panes of a split window, click inside a pane to activate it, or press **F6**.

View—Full Screen

Displays the worksheet window maximized, without the status bar, formula bar, or docked (non-floating) toolbars. To zoom in on a section of a worksheet without hiding these, see "View— Zoom."

1. Open the View menu .... $\boxed{\text{Alt}}$+$\boxed{\text{V}}$

2. Select Full Screen .... $\boxed{\text{U}}$

TIP

To return to a normal viewing screen, press **Esc** or click on the **Full Screen** button.

View—Hiding Cells

Hides rows or columns from view temporarily. To create an outline for analyzing worksheet totals (while hiding detail rows or columns temporarily), see "Outline—Creating."

1. Select the rows or columns you want to hide.

2. Open the Format menu .... Alt + O

3. Select **R**ow or Column .... R or C

4. Select **H**ide .... H

Instead of steps 2–4, press **Ctrl+9**.

TIP

Instead of following steps 2–4, select **Hide** or **Unhide** from the shortcut menu.

MOUSE

You can also hide rows or columns by dragging the right edge of a column to meet the left, or bottom edge of a row to meet the top.

MOUSE

To later unhide rows or columns, open the View menu, select **R**ow or Column, and select **U**nhide, or press **Ctrl+Shift+9**.

TIP

View—Zoom

Displays the worksheet, or a section of it, larger or smaller. To increase or decrease the size of a printed worksheet, see "Page Setup—Page Size and Orientation."

TIP

To zoom in on a chart, be sure that the Sized with Window command on the View menu is *not selected*.

1. **(Optional)** Select a section of the worksheet to zoom in on.

2. Open the View menu .... `Alt`+`V`

3. Select Zoom .... `Z`

4. Select a magnification:

   200 .... `Alt`+`0`

   100 .... `Alt`+`1`

   75 .... `Alt`+`7`

   50 .... `Alt`+`5`

   25 .... `Alt`+`2`

   Fit Selection .... `Alt`+`F`

   Custom .... `Alt`+`C`

   zoompercentage

EXAMPLE

If you select Fit Selection, Excel will size the selected rows or columns to fit the window.

MOUSE

Instead of steps 2–4, select a zoom option from the **Zoom Control** drop-down list box located on the **Standard** toolbar.

View Manager—Adding a View

This Excel 5 add-in saves different views of a worksheet so you can switch between them easily. You can also save and switch between worksheets in the same workbook. To switch between saved views, see "View Manager—Switching Between Views."

TIP

View Manager is an *add-in*; it must be installed before using. If you selected *full installation* when installing Excel, this was done for you; otherwise you can rerun Microsoft Excel Setup to install View Manager.

1. Change the desired Show options.

2. Open the View menu .... Alt + V

3. Select View Manager V

TIP

If the View Manager option is not displayed, see "*Add-ins—Making Add-ins Available.*"

4. Select Add ....[Alt]+[A]

5. Enter a name for the view ....*name*

EXAMPLE

For example, enter **Sheet1:Quarterly Sales Only**.

6. **(Optional)** Change desired settings to save with the view:

   Print Settings ....[Alt]+[P]

   Hidden **R**ows and Columns ....[Alt]+[R]

7. Select **OK**...[↵]

View Manager—Switching Between Views

Switches between saved views. To save a view of a worksheet, see "View Manager—Adding a View."

1. Open the **V**iew menu ....[Alt]+[V]

2. Select **V**iew Manager ....[V]

3. Select a view ....[↑] [↑]

4. Select **S**how ....[↵]

Window—Activating

Activates an open window. To open more than one window, see "Window—New Window." To switch directly to the next window in the list, see "Window—Next Window."

1. Select the Window menu .... **Alt** + **W**

2. Type the number of the
   window you want to activate .... **#**

MOUSE

You can click anywhere on the visible portion of a window to activate it.

Window—Arranging

Rearranges windows on the screen in a preset pattern. See also "Window—Minimizing," "Window—Maximizing," "Window—Moving," and "Window—Sizing."

1. Open the Window menu .... **Alt** + **W**

2. Select Arrange .... **A**

3. Select an option:

   Tiled .... **Alt** + **T**

   Horizontal .... **Alt** + **O**

   Vertical .... **Alt** + **V**

   Cascade .... **Alt** + **C**

4. **(Optional)** To arrange only the active windows of the current workbook, select Windows of Active Workbook .... `Alt`+`W`

5. Select **OK** .... `←`

Window—Closing

Closes the active window. To close the Excel program window (exit Excel), see "Exiting."

1. Open the document's **Control** menu .... `Alt`+`-`

2. Select **Close** .... `C`

MOUSE

Instead of steps 1 and 2, double-click on the document's **Control-menu box**.

TIP

To close a document window quickly, press **Ctrl+F4**.

Window—Freezing

Stops scrolling of the top and left panes of a split window. See "View—Freezing Titles."

Window—Maximizing

Expands a document (worksheet) window to fill the entire screen.

1. Open the document's
   Control menu ....

2. Select Maximize .... 𝗫

MOUSE To maximize a document window quickly, click on the **Maximize button** (upward arrow) in the upper right corner of the document window, or double-click on the window's **title bar**.

To restore the window to the previous size, click on the **Restore button** (two-headed arrow) in the upper right corner of the document window.

TIP To maximize a document window quickly, press **Ctrl+F10**. To restore the window to the previous size, select **Restore** from the document's **Control** menu, or press **Ctrl+F5**.

Window—Minimizing

Collapses the document window to an icon at the bottom of the screen.

1. Open the document's
   Control menu .... 𝐀𝐥𝐭 + −

2. Select Minimize .... 𝗡

MOUSE

To minimize a document window quickly, click on the **Minimize** button (downward arrow) in the upper right corner of the document window.

To restore a document window to its previous size, click on the **Restore** button (two-headed arrow) in the upper right corner of the document window.

TIP

To minimize a document window quickly, press **Ctrl+F9**. To restore the window to the previous size, select **R**estore from the document's **Control** menu, or press **Ctrl+F5**.

Window—Moving

Moves the document window to a new location. (Note: you can't move a maximized window.)

Mouse Steps

1. Point to the document's title bar and click.

2. Drag to a new location, and release the mouse button.

Keyboard Steps

1. Open the document's
   Control menu .... Alt + -

2. Select **M**ove .... M

Instead of steps 1 and 2, press **Ctrl+F7**.

TIP

3. Move the window to
   a new location ....↑ ↑ ← →

4. When the window is in
   the new location, press ....↵

Window—New Window

Creates a new window of the active worksheet, so you can display different portions of one worksheet at the same time. To create a new worksheet, see "Worksheet—New." To arrange open windows, see "Window—Arranging."

Any changes you make to one window will affect the other, but the windows won't scroll together in synch.

TIP

To display different worksheets from the same workbook in different windows, see *"Worksheet—Displaying Multiple Worksheets."*

TIP

1. Select the **W**indow menu ....Alt +W

2. Select New Window ....N

Window—Protecting

Prevents a window from being moved, resized, minimized, maximized, hidden or unhidden.

EXAMPLE

If you have a customized workbook you want to display the same way each time it is opened, use this command.

1. Open the Tools menu .... Alt + T

2. Select **Protection** .... P

3. Select Protect Workbook .... W

4. Select Windows .... Alt + W

5. **(Optional)** Enter a password to prevent this option being changed by the user .... Alt + P

   password

6. Select **OK** .... ↵

TIP

To unprotect windows later, *you must know the password* if you entered one. Open the Tools menu, select Unprotect Workbook, and enter a password if necessary.

Window—Restoring

See "Window—Maximizing" or "Window—Minimizing."

Window—Sizing

Changes the size of a worksheet window.

Mouse Steps

1. Move the mouse pointer to the window border (the mouse pointer will change to a two-headed arrow).

2. Drag the border to the desired size.

Keyboard Steps

1. Open the document's
   Control menu .... `Alt` + `-`

2. Select Size .... `S`

TIP Instead of steps 1 and 2, press **Ctrl+F8**.

3. Size the window .... `↑` `↑` `←` `→`

4. After the window is sized, press .... `↵`

Window—Splitting

*Splits a worksheet window into **panes** so you can see various portions of the document at one time. The window is split at the current cell, into as many as four panes. To freeze row and/or column headings at the same time, see "View—Freezing Titles."*

1. Move to the cell at which point you wish to split the window.

EXAMPLE For example, to split the window so you see columns A to C in the left pane, and columns D, E, etc. in the right pane, move to cell D1. To split the window into four panes, move to a lower cell in column D, such as D5.

2. Open the **Window** menu .... Alt + W

3. Select **Split** .... S

MOUSE To split a window quickly, drag either *split bar* (or both) onto the worksheet. (The split bars are dark black bars at the top of the vertical scroll bar, and the right of the horizontal scroll bar.) To remove a split, drag it off the window. (To split a window exactly in *half*, double-click on the split bar instead of dragging it.)

TIP To unsplit a window, select Remove **Split** from the **Window** menu, or double-click on the split bar.

TIP To move between panes of a split window, click inside a pane to activate it, or press **F6**.

Window—Zooming

See "View—Zoom."

Workbook—Changing the Number of Default Worksheets

When a new workbook is created, it always contains 16 worksheets. Use this command to change that "default" number. In an existing workbook, worksheets can still be added or deleted. See "Worksheet—New" and/or "Worksheet—Deleting."

1. Open the **T**ools menu .... `Alt` + `T`

2. Select **O**ptions .... `O`

3. Move to the **General** tab .... `Ctrl` + `Tab`

4. Change the number of
   default worksheets .... `Alt` + `S`
   number

5. Select **OK**. .... `↵`

Workbook—Closing

Closes the active workbook, and all enclosed worksheets. See "Window—Closing."

Workbook—New

*Creates a **workbook**—a file where all materials related to a common task (charts, worksheets, macros) are stored. When Excel creates a new workbook, by default it contains 16 worksheets.*

These can be deleted, moved, copied, and more can be added. To change the number of default worksheets, see "Workbook—Changing the Number of Default Worksheets."

New workbooks are named consecutively. When you save a workbook for the first time, you may give it a new name. See *"Workbook—Saving"* or *"Workbook—Saving With a New Name."*

For example, a workbook could contain the related worksheets and charts for a single presentation.

EXAMPLE

1. Open the File menu .... Alt + F
2. Select New .... N

Instead of steps 1 and 2, click on the **New Workbook** button on the **Standard** toolbar.

MOUSE

Instead of steps 1 and 2, press **Ctrl+N**.

TIP

Workbook—Opening

Opens an existing workbook. If you have trouble locating the workbook you want, see "File—Finding."

1. Open the File menu .... `Alt`+`F`
2. Select **Open** .... `O`

MOUSE

Instead of steps 1 and 2, click on the **Open** button on the **Standard** toolbar.

TIP

Instead of steps 1 and 2, press **Ctrl+O**.

3. **(Optional)** Change to a different **Drive** .... `Alt`+`V`
   `↑` `↑`

4. **(Optional)** Change to a different **Directory** .... `Alt`+`D`
   `↑` `↑`

5. Select the file (workbook) you wish to open .... `Alt`+`N`
   `Tab`
   `↑` `↑`

TIP

You can also open a workbook in *protected mode*. See *"Workbook—Protecting"* for more information.

6. Select **OK** ....

Workbook—Printing

See "Printing—Workbook."

Workbook—Protecting

Protects data in a workbook so it cannot be changed. To protect a single worksheet, see "Worksheet—Protecting."

1. Open the File menu ....  **Alt** + **F**

2. Select Save **As** .... **A**

Instead of steps 1 and 2, press **F12**.

TIP

3. Select Options .... **Alt** + **O**

4. Enter the desired passwords:

   Protection Password
   Workbook cannot be opened
   without the password .... **Alt** + **P**
   password

   Write Reservation Password
   Workbook cannot be
   saved without the password.
   (Changes can be saved
   under another filename.) .... **Alt** + **W**
   password

Read-Only Recommended
Message will display when
the workbook is opened,
recommending that the
user select *Read Only* from
the Open dialog box ....

5. Select **OK** .... ⏎

6. **(Optional)** If needed, reenter
   the password .... ***password***
   ⏎

7. **(Optional)** If you want,
   enter a new name for the
   workbook .... ***filename.ext***

8. Select **OK**.

9. **(Optional)** If necessary,
   replace the existing workbook
   with the protected version .... Alt + Y

To remove protection later on, *you must
know the password*. Open the workbook
with the password, open the File menu,
select Save **As**, select **O**ptions, and delete
the password. Replace the existing workbook with an unprotected version, and
you're through.

Workbook—Saving

*Saves a workbook file and all its worksheets. To
save a previously-saved workbook with a different*

name, see "Workbook—Saving With a New Name."
To save a group of workbooks together so they
can be opened in a single step, see "Workspace—
Saving."

1. Open the File menu ....

2. Select **Save** .... Ⓢ

MOUSE

Instead of steps 1 and 2, click on the **Save**
button on the **Standard** toolbar.

TIP

Instead of steps 1 and 2, press **Ctrl+S**.

3. Enter a name for the
   workbook ....*filename.ext*

4. **(Optional)** Change to a
   different **Drive** .... Alt + V
   ↑ ↑

5. **(Optional)** Change to a
   different **Directory** .... Alt + D
   ↑ ↑

TIP

You can protect a workbook from further
changes as you save it. See *"Workbook—*
Protecting."

6. **(Optional)** To force Excel to save
   the original *and* changed versions
   of a workbook whenever you save it:

   Select **O**ptions .... Alt + O
   Select Always Create **B**ackup .... Alt + B
   Select **OK**... ⏎

EXAMPLE For example, if you made changes to a
file called SALES93.XLS, when you saved
it, you would have two files:
SALES93.BAK (the unchanged version)
and SALES93.XLS (the changed version).

7. Select **OK**... ⏎

Workbook—Saving With a New Name

*Saves a previously-saved workbook file under a
new name; you will have two copies with different
names. To save a workbook for the first time, see
"Workbook—Saving."*

EXAMPLE If you updated a file called
BUDGET93.XLS with 1994 data, use this
command to save the file with a new
name (such as BUDGET94.XLS) so that
the original 1993 data is also preserved.

1. Open the **F**ile menu .... Alt + F
2. Select Save **A**s .... A

TIP

Instead of steps 1 and 2, press **F12**.

3. Enter a new name
   for the workbook ....*filename.ext*

4. **(Optional)** Change to a
   different **Drive** .... Alt + V
   ↑ ↑

5. **(Optional)** Change to a
   different **Directory** .... Alt + D
   ↑ ↑

TIP

You can protect a workbook from further changes as you save it. See *"Workbook—Protecting."*

6. Select **OK** .... ⏎

Worksheet—Copying

Makes a copy of the selected worksheet, and inserts it into the current (or another) workbook. If you copy a worksheet within the current workbook, it is renamed so the two versions can be told apart—for example, Sheet12 becomes Sheet12 (2). To move a worksheet instead of copying it, see "Worksheet—Moving."

You can copy multiple worksheets at once by selecting them first. See *"Selecting Worksheets."*

TIP

Mouse Steps

1. Select the worksheet(s) you want to copy.

2. Press and hold .... Ctrl

3. Drag the worksheets to their new location.

To copy worksheets into another work-book, make sure that workbook is visible, and simply drag the selected worksheets to its window while pressing **Ctrl**.

MOUSE

Keyboard Steps

1. Select the worksheet(s) you want to copy. (To select more than one worksheet, you must use the mouse.)

2. Open the Edit menu .... Alt + E

3. Select Move or Copy Sheet .... M

4. **(Optional)** Select a different workbook to which to copy the worksheet(s) .... Alt + T

↑ ↑

5. **(Optional)** Select a worksheet
   to copy the selected worksheet(s) ...... Alt + B
   ↑ ↑

6. Select **C**reate a Copy .... Alt + C

7. Select **OK** .... ⏎

Worksheet—Deleting

Removes a document (worksheet) from a workbook.

TIP

You can delete several worksheets at one
time by selecting them first. See *"Selecting
Worksheets."*

1. Move to the worksheet
   you want to delete .... Ctrl + Page Up

2. Open the **E**dit menu .... Alt + E

3. Select De**l**ete Sheet L

MOUSE

Instead of steps 2 and 3, click the right
mouse button while pointing to the
worksheet's tab, and select **Delete** from
the shortcut menu.

Worksheet—Displaying Multiple Worksheets

Displays multiple worksheets on-screen at one time.

1. Select the **W**indow menu .... Alt + W

2. Select **N**ew Window .... N

3. Arrange the windows so
   that both are visible:

   Open the **W**indow menu .... Alt + W
   Select **A**rrange .... A
   Select an option:
   Tiled .... Alt + T
   H**o**rizontal .... Alt + O
   Vertical .... Alt + V
   Cascade .... Alt + C
   Select **OK** .... ↵

4. In the active window,
   switch to a different
   worksheet .... Ctrl + Page Down

Worksheet—Grouping

Selects multiple worksheets as a group for easy formatting, etc. See "Selecting Worksheets."

Worksheet—Hiding

Hides a worksheet from view. To protect a worksheet from changes instead of hiding it, see "Worksheet—Protecting."

TIP

You cannot hide the only worksheet in a workbook with this command. See *"Workbook—Hiding."*

1. Select the worksheet
   you want to hide .... Ctrl + Tab
2. Open the Format menu .... Alt + O
3. Select Sheet .... H
4. Select Hide .... H

TIP

To later unhide a worksheet, open the
Format menu, select Sheet, and select
Unhide. Choose the worksheet you want
to unhide from the list, then select **OK**.

Worksheet—Inserting

See "Worksheet—New."

Worksheet—Moving

*Moves selected worksheets to another place in the
same workbook, or a different workbook. If you
move a worksheet to a workbook which contains a
worksheet with the same name, Excel renames the
moved worksheet. For example, if you move a
worksheet called Sales to a workbook containing a
Sales worksheet, the moved worksheet will be
renamed Sales (2). To copy a worksheet instead of
moving it, see "Worksheet—Copying."*

TIP

Move multiple worksheets at once by selecting them first. See "*Selecting Worksheets.*"

Mouse Steps

1. Select the worksheet(s) you want to move.

2. Drag the worksheets to their new location.

MOUSE

To move worksheets to another workbook, make sure the workbook is visible, then drag the selected worksheets to the workbook window.

Keyboard Steps

1. Select the worksheet(s) you want to move. (To select more than one worksheet, you must use the mouse.)

2. Open the Edit menu .... Alt + E

3. Select **M**ove or Copy Sheet .... M

4. **(Optional)** Select a different workbook to which to move the worksheet(s) .... Alt + T
   ↑ ↑

5. Select **OK**... ⏎

Worksheet—Moving Between

Moves between worksheets in the same workbook. To move the cursor within a worksheet, see "Worksheet—Moving Within."

Mouse Steps

To move to a different worksheet, click on its tab.

To move between worksheets quickly, use the scrolling buttons located on the horizontal scroll bar:

To move	Click on this button
To the next worksheet	Right arrow
To the previous worksheet	Left arrow
To the first worksheet	Left arrow with vertical bar
To the last worksheet	Right arrow with vertical bar
Among several worksheets at once	Press **Shift** as you click

TIP

To display more or fewer worksheet tabs, drag the Tab Split box along the horizontal scroll bar. Double-click on the **Tab Split box** to display the default number of tabs.

Keyboard Steps

1. Press and hold .... Ctrl

2. To move to the next
    worksheet, press .... Page Down
    To move to the previous
    worksheet, press .... Page Up

Worksheet—Moving Within

*Moves the cursor to a different cell in the worksheet.
To move to a different worksheet, see "Worksheet—
Moving Between." To move to a specific cell or
named range, see "Cells—Go To."*

Mouse Steps

To move	Click here
To a visible cell	On the cell itself.
Up one row	Up arrow on vertical scroll bar.
Down one row	Down arrow on vertical scroll bar.
Left one column	Left arrow on horizontal scroll bar.
Right one column	Right arrow on horizontal scroll bar.
Up one screen	Above the scroll box on vertical scroll bar.
Down one screen	Below the scroll box on vertical scroll bar.
Left one screen	To the left of the scroll box on the horizontal scroll bar.

To move	Click here
Right one screen	To the right of the scroll box on the horizontal scroll bar.

MOUSE

To move an approximate distance within the worksheet, drag one of the scroll boxes along its scroll bar.

Keyboard Steps

To move	Press this
Up or down one cell	⬆ or ⬇
Left or right one cell	⬅ or ➡
Up or down one screen	Page Up or Page Down
Left or right one screen	Alt + Page Up or Alt + Page Down
To the beginning of a row	Home
To cell A1	Ctrl + Home
To the last cell with data in this data group	End + ⬆ or ⬇ or ⬅ or ➡
To the last cell with data in the row	End + ↵
To the last cell in the worksheet data area	End + Home

EXAMPLE

Pressing **End+Home** will move you to the last cell in the rectangular area making up the "worksheet data area," whether or not this cell actually contains data. For example, if cells B1, B3, and C2 contained data, then pressing **End+Home** would move you to cell C3, which forms the lower right-hand corner of the "data area." All other End combinations (such as **End+Up Arrow**) move you to a cell which *actually contains data*.

Worksheet—Naming

Renames a worksheet to any name (up to 31 characters). A worksheet's tab displays its named.

1. Move to the worksheet you want to rename .... $\boxed{\text{Ctrl}}+\boxed{\text{Page Down}}$

2. Open the Format menu .... $\boxed{\text{Alt}}+\boxed{\text{O}}$

3. Select **S**heet .... $\boxed{\text{H}}$

4. Select **R**ename .... $\boxed{\text{R}}$

MOUSE

Instead of steps 1–4, double-click on the worksheet's tab, or click with the right mouse button and select **Rename** from the shortcut menu.

5. Enter a new name for the worksheet .... *name*

6. Select **OK** .... $\boxed{\hookleftarrow}$

Worksheet—New

Adds new documents (worksheets) to the current workbook. Added worksheets are named consecutively; to rename a newly inserted worksheet, see "Worksheet—Naming."

TIP

You can insert several worksheets at one time by selecting several existing worksheets first. See *"Selecting Worksheets."*

1. Move to the worksheet *before* which you want to insert the new worksheet .... `Ctrl` + `Page Up`

2. Open the Insert menu. .... `Alt` + `I`

3. Select **W**orksheet .... `W`

MOUSE

Instead of steps 2 and 3, click the right mouse button while pointing to the worksheet tab, and select **Insert** from the shortcut menu.

Worksheet—Printing

See "Printing—Workbook."

Worksheet—Protecting

Protects a single worksheet so that changes cannot be made to it. To protect a workbook, see

*"Workbook—Protecting." To prevent worksheets
from being added to (or deleted from) a workbook,
see "Worksheet—Protecting." To protect individual
cells within a worksheet, see "Cells—Protecting."*

1. Activate the worksheet
   you want to protect .... `Ctrl` + `Page Down`

2. Open the Tools menu .... `Alt` + `T`

3. Select Protection .... `P`

4. Select Protect Sheet .... `P`

5. **(Optional)** Enter a password
   to prevent these options from
   being changed by the user .... `Alt` + `P`
   password

6. Select the appropriate option(s):

   Contents   Prevent changes
   to cells .... `Alt` + `C`

   Objects   Prevent changes
   to objects such as
   a chart, picture, or
   drawn object. .... `Alt` + `O`

   Scenarios   Prevent changes
   to scenarios .... `Alt` + `S`

7. Select OK.. `↵`

Worksheet—Saving

You cannot save a single worksheet. Instead, you save a workbook, which is a collection of worksheets. See "Workbook—Saving." To save a group of workbooks, see "Workspace—Saving."

Worksheet—Selecting

See "Selecting Worksheets."

Worksheet—Selecting Multiple Worksheets

See "Selecting Worksheets."

Workspace—Saving

Saves a group of workbooks together so they can be opened in a single step. To save a single workbook, see "Workbook—Saving."

TIP

Workspace files end in .XLW (workbook files end in .XLS). Instead of workbook data, workspace files contain pointers to that data, and to the workbook's position on-screen when opened.

Instead of grouping workbooks together, you may find it more convenient to insert new worksheets, or copy or move existing worksheets in your current workbook. See "Worksheet—Inserting," "Worksheet—Copying," and "Worksheet—Moving."

1. Open the workbooks
   you want to group. See
   "Workbook—Opening."

2. Open the File menu .... Alt + F

3. Select Save Workspace .... W

4. Enter a name for the
   workspace .... *filename.ext*

5. (Optional) Change to
   a different Drive .... Alt + V
   ↑ ↑

6. (Optional) Change to
   a different Directory .... Alt + D
   ↑ ↑

7. Select OK .... ↵

8. (Optional) If necessary,
   save changes to the
   open workbooks .... ↵

Index

Symbols

(pound signs) in cells, 50
* (asterisk) wildcard character, 60, 86
... (ellipsis), xxiii
? (question mark) wildcard character, 60, 86
[] (square brackets), worksheet names, 95
3-D charts, 35
3-D references in formulas, 92-93
3-D View command (Format menu), 35

A

A:SETUP command, xiv
absolute references
    copying data, 53
    default for macro recording, 125
    formulas, 89-90
accelerator keys, xvi
    Alt+F4 keys (Exit command), 86
    Alt+N keys (Normal Font), 13

Ctrl+1 keys (Cells command), 8
Ctrl+5 keys (Strikethrough style), 13
Ctrl+9 keys (Hide command), 189
Ctrl+accent (') keys (toggling views), 104
Ctrl+B keys (Bold style), 13
Ctrl+C keys (Copy command, 54)
Ctrl+D keys (Fill Down command), 6, 158
Ctrl+F10 keys (Maximize command), 195
Ctrl+F3 keys (defining names), 139
Ctrl+F4 keys (Close command), 194
Ctrl+F5 keys (Restore command), 195
Ctrl+F7 keys (Move command), 197
Ctrl+F8 keys (Size command), 199
Ctrl+F9 keys (Minimize command), 196
Ctrl+I keys (Italic style), 13
Ctrl+minus sign (-) keys (Delete command), 19

Ctrl+O (Open File
command), xxii
Ctrl+P keys (Print
command), 156
Ctrl+plus sign (+) keys
(Insert dialog box), 22
Ctrl+R keys (Fill Right
command), 6, 158
Ctrl+S keys (Save
command), 206
Ctrl+Shift+F3 keys (naming
cells), 138
Ctrl+Shift+Spacebar keys
(Select All button), 8
Ctrl+U keys (Underline
style), 13
Ctrl+V keys (Paste
command), 56
Ctrl+X keys (Cut
command), 56
Ctrl+Z keys (Undo
command), 184
F11 key (charts in separate
documents), 31
F5 key (Go To command), 20
formatting numbers, 15
Shift+F9 keys (Calc Sheet
button), 99
activating
charts, 24
windows, 193
active cells, xx, 24
Add command (Table
menu), 133
Add Criteria command (Criteria
menu), 135
add-ins, 1-3
Microsoft Query, 132
Slideshow, 172
Add-Ins command (Tools
menu), 2

adding
bars/lines to charts, 41-42
borders to cells/worksheets,
8-9
custom buttons to
toolbars, 122
data to charts, 25
macros
to buttons, 121
to toolbars, 122-123
to Tools menu, 123-124
numbers to formulas, 90
records to data lists, 67-68
shortcut keys to menu
commands, 124
text to charts, 47
addresses
absolute/relative
references, 89
cells, xix
Advanced Filter, filtering data
lists, 72-74
aligning cell data, 10-12
Alignment buttons (Formatting
toolbar), 12
Alignment tab, 11, 39
Alt+F4 keys (Exit
command), 86
Alt+N keys (Normal Font), 13
Analysis ToolPak, 1
applets, 85
areas for selection in charts, 46
Arrange command (Window
menu), 94, 193, 211
arranging windows, 193-194
arrow keys, selecting cells with
keyboard, xxvii-xxviii
arrows in charts, 26
Assign Macro command (Tools
menu), 123
asterisk (*) wildcard character, 86

audit tracing
    dependent cells, 3-4
    precedents, 4-5
AutoFill
    cell contents, 5-6
    copying cell formats, 6-7
    creating series of items,
        168-169
AutoFilter
    filtering data lists, 75-76
    see also data lists
AutoFormat, 7, 26
AutoSave add-in, 1
AutoSum, 7-8
AutoSum button (Standard
    toolbar), 8
AVERAGE function, 105
Axes command (Insert
    menu), 27
axis labels for charts, 25-27

B

B:SETUP command, xiv
bars, adding to charts, 41-42
Bold style (Ctrl+B keys), 13
Border tab, 9
borders, adding to cells/
    worksheets, 8-9
Borders button (Formatting
    toolbar), 9
Bring to Front button (Drawing
    toolbar), 107
bringing graphic objects to
    front, 106-107
buttons
    adding macros to, 121
    Alignment (Formatting
        toolbar), 12
    AutoSum (Standard
        toolbar), 8

Borders (Formatting
    toolbar), 9
Bring to Front (Drawing
    toolbar), 107
Calc Now (F9 key), 99
Calc Sheet (Shift+F9 keys), 99
changing properties, 121
ChartWizard (Chart
    toolbar), 33
Color (Formatting
    toolbar), 37
Copy (Standard toolbar), 53
Currency Style (Formatting
    toolbar), 38
custom, adding to
    toolbars, 122
dialog box commands/
    options, xxv
Drawing Selection (Drawing
    toolbar), 111
File Open (Standard
    toolbar), 129
Font Color (Formatting
    toolbar), 37
Font styles (Formatting
    toolbar), 14
Format Painter (Standard
    toolbar), 17
Freeform (Drawing
    toolbar), 108
Full Screen, 189
Function Wizard (Standard
    toolbar), 105
Group Objects (Drawing
    toolbar), 111
Help (Standard toolbar), 116
Maximize, 195
Minimize, 196
Minimize/Maximize, xvi
New Workbook (Standard
    toolbar), 202

number formatting
(Formatting toolbar),
15, 38
Open (Standard toolbar), 203
Paste Link, 65
PivotTable Wizard (Query
and Pivot toolbar), 151
Print Preview (Standard
toolbar), 154
Record Macro (Visual Basic
toolbar), 125
Remove All Arrows (Auditing
toolbar), 3-4
Restore, xvi, 195
Return Data to Excel (Query
and Pivot toolbar), 134
Run Macro (Visual Basic
toolbar), 128
Save (Standard toolbar), 206
Select All, xix, 8
selecting from toolbars, 180
Send to Back (Drawing
toolbar), 114
Stop Macro, 124, 127
Tab scrolling, xx
TipWizard (Standard
toolbar), 178-179
Trace Dependents (Auditing
toolbar), 4-5
Ungroup Objects (Drawing
toolbar), 112

C

Calc Now button (F9 key), 99
Calc Sheet button (Shift+F9
keys), 99
calculating
charts, 27
formulas, 97-99

Calculation tab, 97
cancelling macros, 129
cells
absolute/relative
references, 89
active, xx
addresses, xix
aligning data, 10-12
borders to, 8-9
changing text appearance,
12-14
clearing, 15-17
copying
contents/formats with
Autofill, 5-7
data in, 52
formats, 17-18
formatting to ranges,
157-158
defining names for, 139-140
deleting, 18-19
dependent, audit tracing, 3-4
deselecting, xxvii
displaying active, 24
editing data, 57
flags for notes, 185
formatting, 14-15, 88
Go To command (Edit
menu), 20
hiding, 189-190
inserting copied/cut, 61
inserting in worksheets, 21
multiple, selecting, 166-167
named, in formulas, 103-104
naming, 137-139
pound signs (####) in, 50
precedent, audit tracing, 4-5
protecting, 23
ranges, xxvi
selecting, xxvi-xxviii,
165-166
viewing formulas in, 104

Cells command (Format menu), 8
Cells command (Insert menu), 22
changing margins, 129
Chart tab, 43
Chart toolbar
  Chart Type box, 28
  ChartWizard button, 33
  Horizontal Gridlines tool, 40
  Legend tool, 41
Chart Type command (Format menu), 28
charts
  activating, 24
  adding
    axis labels/data, 25
    lines/bars, 41-42
    text, 47
  arrows, 26
  Autoformatting, 26
  axes labels, 27
  calculating, 27
  chart types, 28
  creating in separate documents, 30
  data labels, 32
  deleting data in, 32
  editing data series, 33
  embedded, 29
  error bars, 34
  formatting, 36-39
  gridlines, 40
  legends, 40-41
  moving, 42
  moving averages, 48
  moving objects, 43
  objects/areas for selection, 46
  pie, exploding, 35
  printing, 43-44
  saving, 162

scaling, 44-45
shadow boxes around, 37
sizing, 46
spell checking, 47
titles, 48
trendlines, 48
types, 28
zooming, 190-191
see also worksheets
ChartWizard button (Chart toolbar), 33
ChartWizard tool (Standard toolbar), 30
check boxes in dialog boxes, xxv
Clear command (Edit menu), 15
clearing cells, 15-17
clicking on items, xxi
Clipboard
  copying data to, 52
  inserting contents, 61
  pasting data, 62
closing
  windows, 194
  workbooks, 201
Color button (Formatting toolbar), 37
color charts, printing, 44
Column command (Format menu), 51
Column heading, xviii
columns
  deleting, 18-19
  hiding, 189-190
  multiple, selecting, 166-167
  selecting, 165-166
  width, 50
command buttons in dialog boxes, xxv
commands
  A:SETUP, xiv

adding shortcut keys to
  menus, 124
B:SETUP, xiv
choosing from menus,
  xxii-xxiii
Criteria menu
  Add Criteria, 135
  Remove All Criteria, 137
Data menu
  Filter, 73
  Form, 67
  Get External Data, 2, 132
  Group and Outline, 142
  Pivot table, 151-153
  Sort, 79
  Subtotals, 80
Edit menu
  Clear, 15
  Copy, 18
  Cut, 55
  Delete, 15, 161
  Delete Sheet, 210
  Fill, 6, 158
  Find, 59-60
  Go To, 20
  Links, 119
  Move or Copy Sheet,
  209, 213
  Paste, 54
  Paste Special, 18, 63-65
  Repeat, 160
  Replace, 65-67
  Undo, 184
  Undo Sort, 79
File menu
  Exit, xxviii, 85-86
  Find File, 86
  New, 172
  Open, 24
  Page Setup, 43, 144-148
  Print, 155

Print Preview, 154-155
Return Data to Microsoft
  Excel, 134
Run, xiv
Save, 206
Save As, 207
Save Workspace, 221
Format menu
  3-D View, 35
  AutoFormat, 7
  Cells, 8
  Chart Type, 28
  Column, 51
  Object, 110
  Placement, 114
  Row, 160
  Style, 176
grayed names, xxii
Help menu, 115-116
Insert menu
  Axes, 27
  Cells, 22
  Data Labels, 32
  Error Bars, 34
  Function, 105
  Gridlines, 40
  Insert Copied/Cut
  Cells, 61
  Legend, 41
  Names, 137
  Object, 84
  Page Break, 144
  Picture, 112
  Remove page Break, 144
  Rows, 162
  Titles, 48
  Trendline, 49
  Worksheet, 218
Options menu, Menu Item
  on Tools Menu, 123
selecting, 129-130

selection letters, xxii
shortcut menu
  3-D View, 35
  AutoFormat, 27
  Chart Type, 28
  Clear Contents, 16
  Delete, 19, 161
  Format Axis, 38, 45
  Format Cells, 9
  Format xxxx Area, 37
  Format xxxx text, 39
  Hide/Unhide, 189
  Insert Data Labels, 32
  Insert Gridlines, 40
  Rename, 217
Table menu, Add
  command, 133
Tools menu
  Add-Ins, 2
  Assign Macro, 123
  Goal Seek, 96
  Macro, 123
  Macro Run, 128
  Options, 97
  Protection, 219
  Record Macro, 124
  Scenarios, 163-164
  Solver, 101
  Spelling, 174-176
Tools menu/Record Macro
  Record at Mark, 127
  Record New Macro
  command, 125
Tools menu/Auditing
  submenu, Remove All
  Arrows/Trace
  Dependents, 3-4
View menu
  Full Screen, 188-189
  Toolbars, 108, 151, 179
  View Manager, 191
  Zoom, 190

WIN, xiv
Window menu
  Arrange, 94, 193, 211
  Freeze Panes, 188
  New Window, 197, 211
  Remove Split, 200
  Split, 200
  Unfreeze Panes, 188
comparision operators, 136
components of Excel 5.0
  screen, xv-xx
Control-menu box, xvi
Copy button (Standard
  toolbar), 53
Copy command (Edit
  menu), 18
copying
  cells
    contents/formats with
      Autofill, 5-7
    formats, 17-18
    formatting to ranges, 157-158
  data in cells, 52
  graphic objects, 107
  worksheets, 208-210
Create Button tool (Drawing
  toolbar), 120-121
Criteria menu commands
  Add Criteria, 135
  Remove All Criteria, 137
Currency Style button
  (Formatting toolbar), 38
custom buttons, adding to
  toolbars, 122
custom filters, 76
Custom Lists tab, 168
customizing toolbars, 179-180
Cut button (Standard
  toolbar), 56
Cut command (Edit menu), 55
cutting and pasting data, 55-56

D

data
    copying, 52
    editing, 57
    formatting, 88
    inserting copied/cut, 61
Data Forms, data lists, 69-70
Data Labels command (Insert menu), 32
data lists
    adding records to, 67-68
    creating, 68-69
    creating pivot tables from, 150-152
    Data Forms, 69-70
    deleting records, 70
    editing records, 71
    extracting data, 82
    filtering, 72-76
    finding a record, 76-78
    sorting, 78-79
    subtotals, 80-82
Data menu commands
    Filter, 73
    Form, 67
    Get External Data, 2, 132
    Group and Outline, 142
    Pivot table, 151-153
    Sort, 79
    Subtotals, 80
data series, editing in charts, 33
data sources in queries, 130-132
databases, extracting data, 82-83
dates, entering in cells, 58
DDE (Dynamic Data Exchange), 117
default worksheets, workbooks, 201

defining
    names for cells/ranges, 139-140
    range names, 157
Delete command (Edit menu), 15, 161
Delete dialog box, 19
Delete Sheet command (Edit menu), 210
deleting
    cells/rows/columns, 18-19
    data in charts, 32
    data list records, 70
    graphic objects, 109
    page breaks, 144
    rows, 161
    worksheets, 210
dependent cells, audit tracing, 3-4
deselecting cells, xxvii
dialog boxes, xxiv-xxv
    Browse, 3
    Chart Type, 29
    Data Form, 69
    Define Name, 140
    Delete, 19
    Edit Slide, 173
    Find File, 87
    Get External Data, 134
    Insert, 22
    New, 172
    Page Setup, 154
    Paste Special, 25
    Print, 154
    Scenario Manager, 164
    Search, 87
    Select Data Source, 131
    Solver Results, 102
    Spelling, 174
    Update Links, 119

displaying
  active cells, 24
  multiple worksheets,
    210-211
  toolbars, 180-182
document windows, moving,
  196-197
documents, creating charts in
  separate, 30
DOS prompt, starting
  Excel, xiv
double-clicking on items, xxi
Drag and Drop, copying/
  moving cells, 63
dragging
  data into charts, 25
  mouse, xxi
  to copy data, 53
drawing objects on charts, see
  graphics objects
Drawing Selection button
  (Drawing toolbar), 111
Drawing Selection tool
  (Drawing toolbar), 121
Drawing toolbar, 108
  Bring to Front button, 107
  Create Button tool, 120-121
  Drawing Selection
    button, 111
  Drawing Selection tool, 121
  Group Objects button, 111
  Send to Back button, 114
  Ungroup Objects button, 112
drop-down lists in dialog boxes,
  xxiv
drop-down palettes in toolbars,
  182-183

E

Edit menu commands
  Clear, 15
  Copy, 18
  Cut, 55
  Delete, 15, 161
  Delete Sheet, 210
  Fill, 6, 158
  Find, 59-60
  Go To, 20
  Links, 119
  Move or Copy Sheet,
    209, 213
  Paste, 54
  Paste Special, 18, 63-65
  Repeat, 160
  Replace, 65-67
  Undo, 184
  Undo Sort, 79
editing
  data in cells, 57
  data series in charts, 33
  embedded objects, 85
  records in data lists, 71
  scenarios, 164
  see also data, editing
ellipsis (...), xxiii
embedded
  charts, 29
  objects, 83-85
  editing, 85
entering data in cells, 58
Error Bars command (Insert
  menu), 34
error bars in charts, 34
Esc key, interrupting running
  macros, 128
Excel
  add-ins, 1-3
  exiting, xxviii, 85-86

icon, xiv
screen components, xv-xx
Setup 1 disk, xiv
starting, xiv-xv
Exit command (File menu),
    xxviii, 85-86
exiting Excel, xxviii, 85-86
exploding pie charts, 35
extracting
    database data, 82-83
    specific records (Microsoft
        Query), 135-137

F

F11 key, charts in separate
    documents, 31
F5 key (Go To command), 20
F9 key (Calc Now button), 99
file extensions, 220
File Find, 86-87
File menu commands
    Exit, xxviii, 85-86
    Find File, 86
    New, 172
    Open, 24
    Page Setup, 43, 144-148
    Print, 155
    Print Preview, 154-155
    Return Data to Microsoft
        Excel, 134
    Run, xiv
    Save, 206
    Save As, 207
    Save Workspace, 221
File Open button (Standard
    toolbar), 129
files
    new, 88, 140
    opening, 88, 141
    saving, 88

workbook, .XLS file
    extensions, 220
workspace, .XLW file
    extension, 220
Fill command (Edit menu), 6,
    158, 170
fill handle, 5
Filter command (Data
    menu), 73
filtering
    custom filters, 76
    data lists
        with Advanced Filter,
            72-74
        with AutoFilter, 75-76
Find and Replace, 88
Find command (Edit menu),
    59-60
Find File button (Open dialog
    box), 87
Find File command (File
    menu), 86
flags as notes for cells, 185
Font Color button (Formatting
    toolbar), 37
Font styles buttons (Formatting
    toolbar), 14
Font tab, 13
footers, 144-145
Form command (Data
    menu), 67
Format Axis command
    (shortcut menu), 45
Format Cells (shortcut menu), 9
Format Cells dialog box,
    Alignment tab, 10-12
Format menu commands
    3-D View, 35
    AutoFormat, 7
    Cells, 8
    Chart Type, 28

Column, 51
Object, 110
Placement, 114
Row, 160
Style, 176
Format Painter button
    (Standard toolbar), 17, 88
Format xxxx Area command
    (shortcut menu), 37
Format xxxx text command
    (shortcut menu), 39
formatting
    3-D chart views, 35
    cells/data, 88
    charts, 36-39
    copying
        cells to ranges, 157-158
        for cells, 17-18
    graphic objects, 109-111
    numbers, 14-15, 140
    text, 13
Formatting toolbar, xix
    Alignment buttons, 12
    Borders button, 9
    Color button, 37
    Currency Style button, 38
    Font Color button, 37
    Font styles buttons, 14
    number formatting buttons,
        15, 38
Formula bar, xix
formulas
    adding numbers, 90
    calculation options, 97-99
    creating, 90-92
    functions, 95
    Goal Seeking, 96-97
    protecting, 97
    references
        3-D, 92-93
        absolute/relative, 89-90
        linked, 94-95

scenarios, 99
Solver, 100-102
totaling, 102
viewing in cells, 104
Freeform button (Drawing
    toolbar), 108
Freeze Panes command
    (Window menu), 188
freezing
    titles, 187-188
    windows, 194
Full Screen command (View
    menu), 188-189
Function command (Insert
    menu), 105
Function Wizard, inserting
    functions into cells,
    104-106
Function Wizard button
    (Standard toolbar), 105
functions
    AVERAGE, 105
    formulas, 95
    inserting into cells with
        Function Wizard, 104-106
    PMT/SUM, 105

G

General tab, 201
Get External Data command
    (Data menu), 2, 132
Go To command (Edit
    menu), 20
Goal Seek command (Tools
    menu), 96
graphic objects
    bringing to front, 106-107
    copying, 107
    creating, 107-109
    deleting, 109

formatting, 109-111

grouping/ungrouping, 111-112

inserting in worksheets, 112

moving, 112-113

selecting, 113

sending to back, 114

sizing/shaping, 114-115

grayed commands, xxii

gridlines in charts, 40

Gridlines command (Insert menu), 40

Group and Outline command (Data menu), 142

Group Objects button (Drawing toolbar), 111

grouping

graphic objects, 111-112

worksheets, 211

H

headers/footers, 144-145

height of rows, 160-161

Help button (Standard toolbar), 116

Help menu commands, 115-116

Hide/Unhide command (shortcut menu), 189

hiding

columns, 189-190

rows, 161

toolbars, 180-182

worksheets, 211-212

Horizontal Gridlines tool (Chart toolbar), 40

horizontal page breaks, 144

I

icon, Excel 5.0, xiv

Insert Data Labels command (shortcut menu), 32

Insert dialog box, 22

Insert Gridlines command (shortcut menu), 40

Insert menu commands

Axes, 27

Cells, 22

Data Labels, 32

Error Bars, 34

Function, 105

Gridlines, 40

Insert Copied/Cut Cells, 61

Legend, 41

Names, 137

Object, 84

Page Break/Remove page Break, 144

Picture, 112

Rows, 162

Titles, 48

Trendline, 49

Worksheet, 218

inserting

Clipboard contents, 61

data in worksheets, 21

functions into cells with Function Wizard, 104-106

graphic objects in worksheets, 112

pictures, 150

rows, 162

interrupting running macros with Esc key, 128

Italic style (Ctrl+I keys), 13

J-K

keyboard
  Autofill cell contents, 6
  choosing menus/commands,
    xxii
  clearing cell contents, 16-17
  data
    copying, 54
    editing, 57
  inserting cells, 22
  moving between/in
    worksheets, 214-217
  running commands, 130
  selecting data,
    xxvii-xxviii, 165

L

labels
  axes of charts, 27
  data, in charts, 32
  entering in cells, 58
  naming cells from, 138-139
Landscape orientation in
  printing, 147
Legend command (Insert
  menu), 41
legends in charts, 40-41
linked
  objects, 84
  references in formulas, 94-95
links, 117-120
Links command (Edit
  menu), 119
list boxes in dialog boxes, xxiv
lists, 75
locating records in data lists,
  76-78

M

Macro command (Tools menu),
  123, 128
macros
  adding
    to buttons, 121
    to toolbars, 121-122
    to Tools menu, 122-123
  cancelling, 129
  interrupting running with
    Esc key, 128
  recording, 124-127
    absolute references as
      default, 125
    pausing, 124
    relative references in, 125
    resuming, 127-128
  running, 126-129
margins, 129, 145-146
Maximize button, 195
Menu bar, xvi
Menu Item on Tools Menu
  command (Options
  menu), 123
menus
  adding shortcut keys to
    commands, 124
  choosing commands from,
    xxii-xxiii
  selection letters, xxii
Microsoft ODBC Support
  Add-in, 1
Microsoft Query, 1
  data sources, 130-132
  extracting specific records,
    135-137
  queries, 132-135
Minimize button, 196
minimizing windows, 195-196

mouse
  Autofill cell contents, 5
  choosing items, xxii
  clearing cell contents, 16
  clicking on items, xxi
  data operations with
    copying, 53
    editing, 57
    selecting, xxvi-xxvii, 165
  inserting cells, 21
  moving between/in
    worksheets, 214-217
  pointing, xxi
  using, xxi
Mouse pointer, xvii
Move or Copy Sheet command
  (Edit menu), 209, 213
moving
  averages in charts, 48
  between worksheets with
    mouse/keyboard, 214-215
  charts, 42-43
  graphic objects, 112-113
  in worksheets, xxv, 215-217
  windows, 196-197
  worksheets, 212-213
multiple
  data, selecting, 166-167
  worksheets, displaying,
    210-211

N

name box, xix
named cells/ranges in formulas,
  103-104
Names command (Insert
  menu), 137
naming
  cells, 137-138

  ranges, 157
  worksheets, 217
navigating worksheets, xxv
New command (File
  menu), 172
new files, 88
New Window command
  (Window menu), 197, 211
new windows, 197
New Workbook button
  (Standard toolbar), 202
Normal Font, Alt+N keys, 13
Number formatting buttons
  (Formatting toolbar),
  15, 38
numbers
  adding to formulas, 90
  formatting, 14-15, 38, 140

O

Object command (Format
  menu), 110
Object command (Insert
  menu), 84
objects
  charts, moving, 43
  embedded, 84-85
  for selection in charts, 46
  graphic
    bringing to front, 106-107
    copying, 107
    creating, 107-109
    deleting, 109
    formatting, 109-111
    grouping/ungrouping,
    111-112
    moving, 112-113
    sending to back, 114
    sizing/shaping, 114-115
  linked, 84

ODBC (Microsoft Open Database Connectivity), 1

OLE (Object Linking and Embedding), 117, 141

Open button (Standard toolbar), 203

Open command (File menu), 24

Open dialog box, Find File button, 87

opening
  files, 88, 141
  workbooks, 141, 202-203

operators, comparision, 136

option buttons in dialog boxes, xxv

Options command (Tools menu), 97

Options menu, Menu Item on Tools Menu command, 123

Options tab, 42

orientation
  in printing, 147
  see also Page Setup command

outline symbols, 142

outlines, 141-143

Page Break command (Insert menu), 144

page breaks, 144

Page Setup command (File menu), 43, 144-148

page size, 150

panes of windows, 199

paper size in printing, 147

passwords in worksheets, 204

Paste command (Edit menu), 54

Paste Link button, 65

Paste Special command (Edit menu), 18, 63-65

Paste Special dialog box, 25

pasting
  data, 55-56
  to Clipboard, 62

Pattern palette, 37

Patterns tab, 39

pausing macro recording, 124

Personal Macro Workbook, 126

Picture command (Insert menu), 112

pictures, 112, 150

pie charts, exploding, 35

Pivot table command (Data menu), 151-153

pivot tables
  creating from data lists, 150-152
  rearranging, 152-153

PivotTable Wizard button (Query and Pivot toolbar), 151

Placement command (Format menu), 114

PMT function, 105

pointing mouse, xxi

Portrait orientation in printing, 147

pound signs (####) in cells, 50

precedent cells and audit tracing, 4-5

preferences in worksheets, 148

Print command (File menu), 155

Print Preview command (File menu), 154-155

printing
  charts, 43-44
  orientation, 147
  paper size, 147

Print Preview, 153-155
specific workbook areas,
    148-150
titles, 155
workbooks, 155-157
properties of buttons,
    changing, 121
protecting
    cells, 23
    formulas, 97
    windows, 198
    workbooks, 204-205
    worksheets, 218-219
Protection command (Tools
    menu), 219
Protection tab, 24
pull-down menus
    Menu bar, xvi
    selecting commands,
        129-130

Q

queries
    creating with Microsoft
        Query, 132-135
    data sources, 130-132
Query and Pivot toolbar
    PivotTable Wizard
        button, 151
    Return Data to Excel
        button, 134
question mark (?) wildcard
    character, 86
quitting Excel program, xxviii

R

ranges
    copying cell formatting,
        157-158
    defining names, 139-140, 157
    filling with series of data,
        169-171
    multiple, selecting, 166-167
    named, 103-104
    naming, 137-138, 157
    of cells, xxvi
rearranging
    pivot tables, 152-153
    windows, 193-194
Rebuild File List check box, 87
Record Macro command (Tools
    menu), 124-127
recording macros, 124-127
    absolute/relative
        references, 125
    pausing, 124
    resuming, 127-128
records
    extracting specific, 135-137
    in data lists
        adding, 67-68
        deleting, 70
        editing, 71
        locating, 76-78
references
    3-D, 92-93
    absolute, 53, 125
    linked, 94-95
    relative
        copying data, 53
        formulas, 89-90
        recording macros, 125
relative operators in
    searches, 77

Remove All Arrows command (Tools menu/Auditing submenu), 3-4

Remove All Criteria command (Criteria menu), 137

Remove page Break command (Insert menu), 144

Remove Split command (Window menu), 200

removing outlines, 143

Rename command (shortcut menu), 217

renaming worksheets, 217

Repeat command (Edit menu), 160

Replace command (Edit menu), 65-67

Report Manager, 1

resizing charts, *see* sizing charts

Restore button, xvi, 195

resuming macro recording, 127-128

Return Data to Microsoft Excel command (File menu), 134

Row command (Format menu), 160

rows
deleting, 18-19, 161
headings, xviii
height, 160-161
hiding, 161, 189-190
inserting, 162
multiple, 166-167
selecting, 165-166

Rows command (Insert menu), 162

Run command (File menu), xiv

Run Macro button (Visual Basic toolbar), 128

running macros, 126-129

S

Save As command (File menu), 207

Save button (Standard toolbar), 206

Save command (File menu), 206

Save Workspace command (File menu), 221

saving
charts, slideshows, 162
files, 88
workbooks, 205-207
workspace, 220-221

Scale tab, 45

scaling charts, 44-45

scenarios in formulas, 99

Scenarios command (Tools menu), 163-164

screens, Excel 5.0 components, xv-xx

scroll arrows/bars/box, xvii

search criteria for data lists, 77

Search dialog box, 87

Select All button, xix, 8

selecting
commands, 129-130
graphic objects, 113
multiple items, 166-167
toolbar buttons, 180
worksheets, 167-168

selection handles, 47

selection letters for menus/ commands, xxii

Send to Back button (Drawing toolbar), 114

separate documents, creating charts in, 30

series of data, 169-171

setting page size, 150
Setup 1 disk (Excel 5.0), xiv
shadow boxes around
    charts, 37
shaping graphic objects,
    114-115
Sheet tab, xx, 148
Shift+F9 keys (Calc Sheet
    button), 99
shortcut keys, *see*
    accelerator keys
shortcut menus, xx, 172
    commands, 129
        3-D View, 35
        AutoFormat, 27
        Chart Type, 28
        Clear Contents, 16
        Delete, 19, 161
        Fill Formats, 7
        Format Axis, 38, 45
        Format Cells, 9
        Format text, 39
        Hide/Unhide, 189
        Insert Data Labels, 32
        Insert Gridlines, 40
        Rename, 217
showing toolbars, 180-182
sizing
    charts, 46
    graphic objects, 114-115
    windows, 199
slide shows, 2, 172-174
Solver Add-in, 2
Solver command (Tools menu),
    101-102
Sort button (Standard toolbar), 80
Sort command (Data menu), 79
sorting data lists, 78
spelling, checking in charts, 47
Spelling command (Tools
    menu), 174-176

Split box, xvii
Split command (Window
    menu), 200
splitting windows, 199-200
square brackets ([]), worksheet
    names, 95
Standard toolbar, xix
    buttons
        AutoSum, 8
        Cut, 56
        File Open, 129
        Format Painter, 17
        Function Wizard, 105
        Help, 116
        New Workbook, 202
        Open, 203
        Print Preview, 154
        Repeat, 160
        Save, 206
        Sort, 80
        TipWizard, 178-179
        Undo, 79
    ChartWizard tool, 30
    Spelling tool, 174
    Zoom Control drop-down list
        box, 191
starting
    charts, 24
    Excel 5.0, xiv-xv
Status bar, xvii
Stop Macro button, 124, 127
Strikethrough style (Ctrl+5
    keys), 13
Style command (Format
    menu), 176
styles, 176-178
Subtotals command (Data
    menu), 80
Subtype tab, 29
SUM function, 105

switching views with View
   Manager, 192
symbols, outline, 142

T

Tab split box, xx
Table menu, Add
   command, 133
tabs
   Alignment, 10-12, 39
   Border, 9
   Calculation, 97
   Chart, 43
   Custom Lists, 168
   Font, 13
   General, 201
   Header/Footer, 144
   Margins, 145
   Number, 14, 38
   Options, 42
   Patterns, 39
   Protection, 24
   Scale, 45
   Sheet, 148
   sheets, xx
   Subtype, 29
   Type, 49
   View, 104, 184-185
   Y Error Bars, 34
tear-off palettes in toolbars,
   182-183
text
   adding to charts, 47
   changing appearance in
      cells, 12-14
   formatting in charts, 38-39
text boxes in dialog
   boxes, xxiv
three-key sorts, data lists, 78

TipWizard button (Standard
   toolbar), 178-179
Title bar, xvi
titles
   charts, 48
   freezing, 187-188
   printing, 155
Titles command (Insert
   menu), 48
toggling views, Ctrl + accent (')
   keys, 104
toolbars
   custom buttons/macros,
      122-123
   customizing, 179-180
   drop-down palettes, 182-183
   selecting buttons, 180
   showing/hiding, 180-182
Toolbars command (View
   menu), 108, 151, 179
Tools menu
   adding macros to, 123-124
   commands
      Add-Ins, 2
      Assign Macro, 123
      Auditing submenu, 3-4
      Goal Seek, 96
      Macro, 123, 128
      Options, 97
      Protection, 219
      Record Macro, 124-127
      Scenarios, 163-164
      Solver, 101
      Spelling, 174-176
ToolTip box, 183
totaling formulas, 102
Trace Dependents button
   (Auditing toolbar), 4-5
trendlines in charts, 48-49
Type tab, 49

U

Underline style (Ctrl+U keys), 13
Undo button (Standard
    toolbar), 79
Undo command (Edit
    menu), 184
Undo Sort command (Edit
    menu), 79
unfiltering lists, 75
Unfreeze Panes command
    (Window menu), 188
Ungroup Objects button
    (Drawing toolbar), 112
updating links, 118-120
using mouse, xxi

V

values, entering in cells, 58
vertical page breaks, 144
View Manager, 2
View menu commands
    Full Screen, 188-189
    Toolbars, 108, 151, 179
    View Manager, 191
    Zoom, 190
View tab, 104, 184-185
viewing
    formulas in cells, 104
    scenarios, 164
    worksheets, 184-187
views
    3-D charts, 35
    switching, 192
    toggling, 104
Visual Basic toolbar
    Record Macro button, 125
    Run Macro button, 128

W

width of columns, 50
wildcard characters
    file finding, 86
    Find command, 60
    searches, 77
WIN command, xiv
Window menu commands
    Arrange, 94, 193, 211
    Freeze Panes, 188
    New Window, 197, 211
    Split/Remove Split, 200
    Unfreeze Panes, 188
windows
    activating, 193
    closing/freezing, 194
    Help, 116
    maximizing/minimizing/
        moving, 195-197
    new, 197
    protecting, 198
    rearranging, 193-194
    sizing, 199
    splitting, 199-200
    zooming, 201
Windows Clipboard
    copying data to, 52
    pasting data, 62
Windows Program
    Manager, xiv
Wizards, xxiv
workbook files, .XLS file
    extensions, 220
workbooks, xv, 201-202
    closing, 201
    new, 140
    opening, 141, 202-203
    printing, 155-157

printing specific areas,
148-150
protecting, 204-205
saving, 162, 205-207
saving with new names,
207-208
worksheet defaults, 201
Workgroup toolbar, Scenarios
drop-down list, 164
Worksheet command (Insert
menu), 218
worksheets, 167-168, 218
adding borders, 8
copying/deleting, 208-210
going directly to cells, 20
grouping, 211
hiding, 211-212
in workbooks, xv
inserting cells/rows/ranges/
columns, 21
inserting graphic objects/
pictures, 112
moving, 212-213
moving between with
mouse/keyboard, 214-215
moving in with mouse/
keyboard, 215-217
multiple, 210-211
names in square brackets
([]), 95
naming/renaming, 217
navigating, xxv
passwords, 204
protecting, 218-219
show options, 185-187
views, 184
workbook defaults, 201
zooming, 190-191
workspace, saving, 220-221
workspace filesl, .XLW file
extension, 220

X-Z

.XLS file extension, workbook
files, 220
.XLW file extension, workspace
files, 220

Y Error Bars tab, 34

Zoom command (View
menu), 190
Zoom Control drop-down list
box (Standard toolbar), 191
zooming
windows, 201
worksheets, 190-191